A Desert Jewel

A Desert Jewel

Dubai's Vibrant Tapestry

Maria M

Mohammed Altaf Hussain

CONTENTS

Table of Content

Introduction: The Oasis Emerges

1. Introduction to Dubai's humble beginnings as a small fishing and trading village.
2. Exploration of the geographical and historical context that led to the city's development.
3. Early cultural influences and the emergence of Dubai as a regional hub.

Chapter 1: "From Sand to Skyscrapers"
1.1 The transformative era of oil discovery and economic boom.
1.2 The visionary leadership that propelled Dubai into a global city.
1.3 The iconic architectural marvels that define the city's skyline.

Chapter 2: "Cultural Kaleidoscope"
2.1 Exploration of Dubai's diverse cultural landscape.
2.2 Celebration of the city's tolerance and inclusivity.
2.3 The role of cultural institutions, festivals, and events in shaping Dubai's identity.

Chapter 3: "Trade and Innovation Hub"
3.1 Dubai's strategic location as a global business and trade center.
3.2 The evolution of free zones and their impact on economic growth.
3.3 Innovations in technology and sustainability that drive the city's progress.

Chapter 4: "The Desert Blooms: Green Initiatives"
4.1 Dubai's commitment to sustainability and environmental conservation.
4.2 Landscaping and greening projects that challenge the desert stereotype.
4.3 Renewable energy initiatives and their impact on the city's future.

Chapter 5: "Luxury and Leisure"
5.1 The rise of Dubai as a luxury destination.

Introduction

The Oasis Emerges

In the core of the Bedouin Desert lies a cutting edge wonder, a city that resists the restrictions of creative mind and designing - Dubai. When a humble fishing and exchanging settlement, Dubai has risen up out of the huge scope of sand as a world-wide symbol of richness, development, and flourishing. This city, with its shining high rises, sumptuous retreats, and aggressive undertakings, has become inseparable from innovation, filling in as a demonstration of the groundbreaking force of human vision and desire.

Dubai's transient ascent can be compared to the development of a desert spring amidst a dry desert. It remains as a demonstration of the flexibility and genius of a country that has tackled its geological difficulties to make a safe house of flourishing. The city's change from a fruitless scene to a worldwide financial center has been completely remarkable, reflecting the incredible development of a desert garden in the midst of the brutal desert conditions.

At the core of Dubai's example of overcoming adversity lies its essential area and visionary authority. Arranged at the intersection of East and West, Dubai has generally been a blend of societies, an exchanging center point where dealers from different corners of the world met to trade products and thoughts. In ongoing many years, Dubai enjoys utilized this verifiable benefit, developing into a worldwide business and the travel industry center point that draws in large number of guests every year.

The dynamic embroidered artwork of Dubai is woven from strings of custom and advancement. The city's horizon is a demonstration of its unflinching obligation to development and progress, with famous designs, for example, the Burj Khalifa puncturing the sky. At the same time, Dubai has painstakingly safeguarded its social legacy, making an agreeable mix of old and new that resounds all through the city's design, food, and way of life.

As the sun sets over the Bedouin Desert, Dubai wakes up with a kaleidoscope of lights and exercises. The city's dynamic nightlife, elite diversion choices, and cutting edge engineering enthrall the faculties, bringing inhabitants and travelers into a domain where conceivable outcomes appear to be boundless. The juxtaposition of custom and advancement in Dubai's social texture makes an exceptional climate, where legacy is praised without repressing the soul of progress.

The financial scene of Dubai reflects its dynamic urbanity. When dependent on oil incomes, the city has broadened its economy, changing into an information put together center with a concentration with respect to areas like money, innovation, and the travel industry.

The visionary administration of the decision government plays had an essential impact in directing Dubai towards reasonable development and improvement. The presentation of free zones, business-accommodating approaches, and key interests in framework has drawn in worldwide organizations and business visionaries the same, transforming Dubai into a worldwide monetary force to be reckoned with.

One can't examine Dubai without wondering about the daring tasks that dab its scene. The Palm Jumeirah, a counterfeit archipelago looking like a palm tree, remains as a demonstration of Dubai's capacity to reshape nature in quest for engineering greatness. The Dubai Shopping center, an epic shopping and diversion complex, is a microcosm of the city's obligation to offering unrivaled encounters. These ventures not just reclassify the restrictions of designing and configuration yet in addition mirror Dubai's desire to be at the very front of worldwide development.

Dubai's obligation to supportability is clear in the structural wonders that effortlessness its horizon. The city has embraced eco-accommodating practices, with drives, for example, the Dubai Reasonable City setting new norms for naturally cognizant metropolitan preparation. As the world wrestles with the difficulties of environmental change, Dubai's proactive methodology towards maintainability positions it as a trailblazer in dependable metropolitan turn of events.

The friendliness area in Dubai is a microcosm of the city's obligation to greatness. Extravagance resorts like the Burj Al Middle Easterner, frequently alluded to as the main seven-star lodging on the planet, rethink lavishness and friendliness guidelines. From the entrancing desert resorts to the modern submerged inns, Dubai's cordiality contributions take care of a different cluster of tastes, giving guests a remarkable encounter that flawlessly mixes solace and excess.

Past the fabulousness and marvelousness, Dubai is a social blend that embraces variety. The city's ostracize populace adds to its cosmopolitan air, uniting individuals from various corners of the globe. This social variety is reflected in Dubai's culinary scene, where conventional Emirati dishes coincide with global flavors, making a gastronomic embroidery that reflects the city's multicultural character.

The development of Dubai as a worldwide social and creative center point adds one more layer to its dynamic embroidery. The Dubai Show, a shocking structural magnum opus, has exhibitions going from old style to contemporary, drawing in craftsmen and crowds from around the world. Workmanship displays, live performances, and far-reaching developments add to Dubai's developing standing as a center for innovativeness and articulation.

As Dubai keeps on advancing, it faces the difficulties that go with quick development and improvement. Issues like metropolitan maintainability, social equity, and social safeguarding request cautious thought to guarantee that the city's advancement stays comprehensive and reasonable.

The administration of Dubai has shown a readiness to address these difficulties, executing strategies and drives pointed toward cultivating an agreeable and adjusted future for the city.

1. **Introduction to Dubai's humble beginnings as a small fishing and trading village.**

   In the tremendous scope of the Bedouin Desert, where vast ridges stretch as may be obvious, lies the cutting edge city of Dubai. While today it remains as a demonstration of human development and structural ability, the city's process is established in the modest starting points of a little fishing and exchanging town. Dubai's change from an unobtrusive settlement on the shores of the Middle Eastern Bay to a worldwide financial force to be reckoned with is a story that interlaces history, culture, and the dauntless soul of its kin.

   Hundreds of years before the transcending high rises and sumptuous hotels enhanced the horizon, Dubai was a spot on the guide, known for its essential area along the shipping lanes that associated the East toward the West. The district's unforgiving desert conditions were tempered by the waters of the Bedouin Bay, giving a life saver to the rise of a little settlement that would ultimately reclassify the idea of metropolitan turn of events.

   Verifiable records demonstrate that as soon as the eighteenth hundred years, Dubai was a crucial general store. Settled along the waterfront strip, the town flourished with the rich marine assets of the Inlet. Fishing turned into a lifestyle for the early occupants, supporting them through the challenging states of the desert. The geological situating of Dubai made it an ideal port for vessels participated in oceanic exchange, working with the trading of merchandise going from pearls and flavors to materials and pottery.

   Dubai's modest starting points were described by the effortlessness of its residences and the interconnectedness of its local area. The engineering of the early town mirrored the functional necessities of its inhabitants, with low-ascent structures developed from neighborhood materials. The twisted rear entryways and yards reflected a general public that put esteem on mutual residing, where families and neighbors shared the difficulties and wins of day to day existence.

   As the nineteenth century unfurled, Dubai's importance as an exchanging center developed, drawing in traders from adjoining locales and then some. The sea exchange, especially in pearls, turned into the financial spine of the town. The pearl plunging industry, a hazardous yet worthwhile undertaking, drew jumpers from different societies, adding to the multicultural embroidery that would later turn into a characterizing element of Dubai.

The customary dhow, a wooden cruising vessel meaningful of Bedouin sea legacy, turned into the life saver of Dubai's exchange. These vessels, with their particular three-sided sails, cruised across the Bay, associating Dubai to ports in India, Persia, and East Africa.

The dhow exchange worked with business as well as established the groundwork for the cosmopolitan idea of Dubai, as it cultivated social trades that made a permanent imprint on the developing personality of the town.

The turn of the twentieth century denoted a crucial crossroads in Dubai's set of experiences. The revelation of oil in the Middle Eastern Landmass proclaimed a time of significant change, changing the financial scene and giving the means to the acknowledgment of excellent aspirations. Nonetheless, Dubai's excursion to thriving was not exclusively dependent on the dark gold that lay underneath its sands; it was an essential vision and insightful initiative that would shape the predetermination of the city.

Dubai's rulers, perceiving the limited idea of oil assets, imagined a future that rose above reliance on a solitary ware. Sheik Rashid receptacle Saeed Al Maktoum, a visionary chief who rose to control in 1958, assumed a crucial part in guiding Dubai towards a direction of financial broadening and modernization. His premonition laid the basis for the city's change into a worldwide center point of trade, money, and the travel industry.

The development of Port Rashid in 1972 denoted a huge achievement in Dubai's development. The profound water port improved the productivity of sea exchange as well as situated Dubai as a significant player in the worldwide transportation industry. The income created from the port, combined with the ground breaking arrangements of Sheik Rashid, established the groundwork for the city's financial versatility.

As the income from oil and exchange filled Dubai, visionary pioneers reinvested it into aggressive framework projects. Sheik Rashid's child, Sheik Mohammed container Rashid Al Maktoum, who accepted authority in 2006, proceeded with the tradition of advancement and progress. The making of the Jebel Ali Free Zone, a business-accommodating territory, pulled in worldwide partnerships and set up for Dubai's development as a worldwide business center point.

The venturesome vision of Dubai arrived at new levels with the development of the famous Burj Al Middle Easterner in 1999, a lavish lodging that became inseparable from richness and building wonder. This was trailed by the culmination of the Burj Khalifa, the world's tallest structure, in 2010, representing Dubai's climb to phenomenal levels on the worldwide stage. These milestones reshaped the city's horizon as well as highlighted Dubai's obligation to pushing the limits of plausibility.

Dubai's financial expansion procedure reached out to the improvement of the travel industry, an area that has since turned into a foundation of its thriving. The development of counterfeit islands, like the Palm Jumeirah and The World, exhibited Dubai's inclination for aggressive tasks intended to catch the world's creative mind.

The city's tireless quest for greatness in cordiality and diversion changed it into an objective that coaxes voyagers from each side of the globe.

The multiculturalism woven into the texture of Dubai is a demonstration of its set of experiences as a general store and sea center. Today, the city remains as a mixture of societies, with ostracizes from around the world calling it home. The multicultural character of Dubai isn't simply an outcome of monetary success yet a purposeful work to cultivate a comprehensive society that celebrates variety.

Dubai's obligation to safeguarding its social legacy is clear in the conservation of notable locales, for example, Al Fahidi Stronghold, which houses the Dubai Historical center. The juxtaposition of the old and the new is a repetitive subject in Dubai, where conventional souks coincide with modern shopping centers, and old practices track down articulation close by state of the art innovation.

2. **Exploration of the geographical and historical context that led to the city's development.**

To grasp the wonder that is cutting edge Dubai, one should set out on an excursion through the geological and verifiable embroidery that established the groundwork for the city's turn of events. Arranged on the southeastern corner of the Bedouin Landmass, Dubai possesses an essential situation along the shore of the Middle Eastern Bay. The city's development is profoundly weaved with the topographical elements of the district, forming its predetermination as an exchanging center point, monetary force to be reckoned with, and structural wonder.

The Bedouin Landmass, portrayed by huge stretches of dry desert, could appear to be a far-fetched origin for a flourishing city. Notwithstanding, Dubai's advancement is characteristically connected to the accessibility of water, explicitly the waters of the Bedouin Bay. The presence of this tremendous waterway gave a life saver to the early occupants of the locale, considering food through fishing and cultivating oceanic exchange that laid the basis for Dubai's rise.

The seaside area of Dubai made it a characteristic harbor, offering cover for ships participated in sea exchange. This topographical benefit worked with the connection of different societies and the trading of products from as soon as the eighteenth 100 years. The protected waters of the Inlet turned into the preparation reason for gifted mariners and pearl jumpers, adding to the sea legacy that would later characterize the personality of Dubai.

Dubai's verifiable roots as a fishing and exchanging town date back to when the district was meagerly populated, and the desert scene extended continuous for a significant distance.

The earliest occupants of the area were Bedouin clans, roaming individuals who explored the difficult landscape of the Middle Eastern Desert. Nonetheless, the beach front settlements, including Dubai, were bound to turn out to be something other than occasional places to stay.

The essential area of Dubai along antiquated shipping lanes turned out to be progressively evident as sea exchange thrived in the nineteenth hundred years. The town, when dependent on fishing and pearl plunging, changed into an energetic general store, drawing in vendors from Persia, India, and East Africa. The clamoring souks (markets) of Dubai became centers of trade, where merchandise going from flavors and materials to valuable metals and gemstones were traded.

The sea exchange, worked with by the notable dhows, wooden cruising vessels with particular three-sided sails, associated Dubai to far off ports and laid out it as an essential hub in the local exchange organization. These vessels, crossing the waters of the Inlet, were channels for products as well as transporters of social trade, encouraging a cosmopolitan air that would persevere as the centuries progressed.

As the twentieth century unfolded, Dubai ended up at the intersection of progress. The disclosure of oil in the Bedouin Promontory carried freshly discovered abundance to the locale, modifying the monetary scene and making way for Dubai's quick change. While oil would later turn into an impetus for the city's development, it was the visionary initiative of Sheik Rashid canister Saeed Al Maktoum, who expected power in 1958, that guided Dubai towards broadening and modernization.

Perceiving the limited idea of oil assets, Sheik Rashid set out on an aggressive excursion to situate Dubai as a worldwide financial player. The income produced from oil trades was decisively reinvested into framework extends that established the groundwork for the city's future thriving. The development of Port Rashid in 1972, a profound water port equipped for taking care of huge vessels, upgraded Dubai's oceanic capacities as well as represented the city's obligation to turning into a vital participant in the worldwide delivery industry.

At the same time, Sheik Rashid's child, Sheik Mohammed container Rashid Al Maktoum, who accepted administration in 2006, proceeded with the tradition of his dad. The formation of the Jebel Ali Free Zone, laid out in 1985, denoted an essential second in Dubai's financial expansion. This business-accommodating territory pulled in worldwide enterprises and laid the preparation for Dubai's rise as a worldwide business and coordinated factors center.

Dubai's topographical benefit stretched out past its waterfront area. The huge deserts that encompass the city, at first saw as hindrances to advancement, became materials for venturesome undertakings that would catch the world's consideration.

The Dubai government's obligation to development and desire appeared in undertakings, for example, the Palm Jumeirah, a counterfeit archipelago molded like a palm tree, and The World, an archipelago of islands addressing a guide of the world. These ventures displayed Dubai's designing ability as well as represented its capacity to reshape nature in quest for great dreams.

The Burj Al Bedouin, finished in 1999, and the Burj Khalifa, finished in 2010, stand as famous tourist spots that accentuate Dubai's horizon. These building wonders, brought into the world from a marriage of vision and designing greatness, epitomize Dubai's obligation to pushing the limits of plausibility. The Burj Khalifa, taking off to uncommon levels, is a demonstration of Dubai's desire to be perceived as a provincial force to be reckoned with as well as a worldwide image of progress.

The authentic and topographical setting of Dubai's advancement is deficient without recognizing the multiculturalism that characterizes the city. The historical backdrop of sea exchange and the union of societies in the beginning of the town established the groundwork for the cosmopolitan idea of current Dubai. Today, the city is home to a different populace, with ostracizes from around the world adding to its multicultural embroidery.

Dubai's obligation to safeguarding its social legacy is apparent in the protection of authentic destinations, for example, Al Fahidi Post, which houses the Dubai Exhibition hall. The juxtaposition of the old and the new is a common subject in Dubai, where conventional souks coincide with modern shopping centers, and old practices track down articulation close by state of the art innovation. This conscious work to keep an association with the past while rushing towards what's in store mirrors Dubai's obligation to a reasonable and comprehensive turn of events.

3. **Early cultural influences and the emergence of Dubai as a regional hub.**

Dubai's development into a worldwide city isn't simply a story of monetary development and compositional wonder; it is likewise an account well established in the social impacts that have formed the personality of this exceptional city. The early social impacts that laid the foundation for Dubai's development as a provincial center point are a mosaic of customs, exchange, and cosmopolitanism.

The social embroidery of Dubai started to come to fruition in the eighteenth century when the town, settled along the shore of the Middle Eastern Bay, changed from an unassuming fishing and exchanging settlement into an energetic oceanic center point. The geological area of Dubai at the junction of East and West situated it as a mixture of societies, a gathering point where dealers and mariners from different districts merged, carrying with them a rich embroidery of customs.

The sea shipping lanes that went through the waters of the Bedouin Bay associated Dubai to far off terrains like India, Persia, and East Africa. The clamoring souks of Dubai became commercial centers where shippers exchanged flavors, materials, pearls, and different items, cultivating a social trade that established the groundwork for the cosmopolitan personality of the city. The customary dhow, with its particular three-sided sails, became a vessel for exchange as well as an image of the interconnectedness of societies.

The pearl jumping industry, which prospered in the nineteenth hundred years, further enhanced Dubai's social texture. Talented jumpers from different social foundations wandered into the profundities of the Bedouin Bay, raising valuable pearls that would be exchanged along the sea courses. The different networks that partook in pearl plunging added to the multiculturalism that would turn into a characterizing element of Dubai in the a very long time to come.

The Bedouin legacy of the early occupants likewise assumed a critical part in molding Dubai's way of life. The Bedouins, itinerant individuals who crossed the huge breadths of the Bedouin Desert, carried with them a bunch of customs and values that underscored flexibility, creativity, and a profound association with the land. While the waterfront and desert ways of life might appear to be divergent, they coincided in Dubai, making a novel mix that recognizes the city's social character.

The appearance of the twentieth century carried massive changes to Dubai, driven by both inner and outside factors. The revelation of oil in the Bedouin Promontory denoted a defining moment, pushing Dubai into another period of financial thriving. The newly discovered abundance empowered the city to leave on aggressive frame-work ventures and modernization endeavors, drawing in a developing exile populace that would additionally enhance Dubai's social scene.

The visionary authority of Sheik Rashid container Saeed Al Maktoum, who ex-pected power in 1958, assumed a critical part in directing Dubai towards turning into a local center point. Sheik Rashid perceived the significance of financial broadening, understanding that the limited idea of oil assets required a more extensive procedure for supported development. The development of Port Rashid in 1972 and the founda-tion of the Jebel Ali Free Zone in 1985 were key achievements that upgraded Dubai's situation as a sea and business center, drawing in individuals from around the world.

Dubai's development as a provincial center was additionally moved by the ground breaking strategies of its chiefs. The production of free zones, which offered charge motivators and smoothed out business processes, pulled in global enterprises and business visionaries. This convergence of unfamiliar ability carried with it a heap of social impacts, changing Dubai into a dynamic and cosmopolitan city.

The change of Dubai's horizon in the late twentieth and mid 21st hundreds of years is a demonstration of the city's obligation to development and progress.

The development of famous designs like the Burj Al Bedouin and the Burj Khalifa reshaped the actual scene as well as became images of Dubai's rising to worldwide noticeable quality. These building wonders, impacted by both customary Bedouin plan and contemporary style, exemplify the combination of old and new that portrays Dubai's social ethos.

The obligation to protecting social legacy in the midst of fast modernization is obvious in drives, for example, the rebuilding of notable destinations like Al Fahidi Stronghold, which currently houses the Dubai Historical center. The juxtaposition of the old and the new is a conscious work to keep an association with the past while embracing the future, making an agreeable mix that characterizes Dubai's social story.

The multiculturalism that saturates Dubai is unmistakable in its regular daily existence, from the dialects expressed in the city to the assorted culinary contributions. The city's exile populace, drawn from north of 200 identities, adds to an energetic and comprehensive social texture. Dubai's obligation to variety is revered in its strategies, cultivating a climate where individuals from various foundations reside and work amicably.

The social schedule of Dubai is rich and different, mirroring the city's obligation to advancing expressions and customs. The Dubai Drama, an elite scene for performing expressions, has a bunch of comprehensive developments, from old style shows to contemporary exhibitions. Craftsmanship exhibitions, live performances, and culinary occasions add to a powerful social scene that takes care of the two occupants and guests.

The culinary scene of Dubai reflects its multicultural character. From customary Emirati dishes to worldwide cooking styles, the city's gastronomic contributions take care of different preferences. The zest scented demeanor of the customary souks mixes with the fragrance of global flavors, making a culinary embroidery that reflects the cosmopolitanism of the city.

Dubai's obligation to social variety stretches out to instruction, with organizations that give a stage to the trading of thoughts and information. The city's scholastic scene invites understudies and researchers from around the world, encouraging a climate of scholarly improvement that rises above borders. The Dubai Worldwide Film Celebration, the Emirates Carrier Celebration of Writing, and other widespread developments add to a powerful intelligent environment.

Chapter 1

"From Sand to Skyscrapers"

In the records of metropolitan turn of events, not many stories reverberate with the greatness and dauntlessness as that of Dubai - a city that rose up out of the grains of desert sand to contact the sky with its famous high rises. The change of Dubai from an unassuming fishing and exchanging town to a worldwide city is an adventure that typifies the unyielding soul of human desire, visionary initiative, and the determined quest for progress. The expression "From Sand to High rises" exemplifies the actual change of the scene as well as the development of a city that challenged geological limitations to turn into an image of advancement and innovation.

Dubai's process starts in the mid eighteenth century when it was an unassuming settlement along the shoreline of the Bedouin Bay. Settled in the midst of the huge region of the Bedouin Desert, the town flourished with fishing and sea exchange. The warm waters of the Inlet not just supported the occupations of the early occupants yet additionally laid the basis for the city's future as an oceanic and exchange center. The customary dhows, with their particular three-sided sails, turned into the vessels that associated Dubai to the far off corners of the world, encouraging social trade and monetary thriving.

As the twentieth century unfolded, the revelation of oil in the Middle Eastern Landmass proclaimed a seismic change in Dubai's fortunes. The recently discovered abundance from oil trades gave the necessary resources to leave on aggressive foundation activities and modernization endeavors. Notwithstanding, the visionary heads of Dubai, especially Sheik Rashid container Saeed Al Maktoum, perceived that oil was a limited asset, and the city's future relied upon enhancement.

The development of Port Rashid in 1972 denoted an essential second in Dubai's change. The profound water port worked with sea exchange as well as situated Dubai as a critical player in the worldwide delivery industry. The income created from oil and exchange was decisively reinvested into additional turn of events, making way for the city's climb to provincial and worldwide noticeable quality.

The daring vision of Dubai's chiefs stretched out past ordinary reasoning. The desert scene that encompassed the city, at first saw as an impediment, turned into the material for visionary activities that would reclassify the city's horizon. The Palm Jumeirah, a counterfeit archipelago looking like a palm tree, and The World, an archipelago of islands looking like a guide of the world, are demonstration of Dubai's capacity to reshape nature in quest for engineering magnificence.

Notwithstanding, it was in the late twentieth and mid 21st hundreds of years that Dubai really caught the world's creative mind with its unrivaled horizon. The notorious Burj Al Middle Easterner, standing like a sail in the ocean, turned into an image of plushness and extravagance when it opened its entryways in 1999. The Burj Khalifa, finished in 2010, remains as the world's tallest structure, penetrating the sky at a level that appeared to be unfathomable only years and years sooner. These design wonders are not just designs of steel and glass yet landmarks that encapsulate Dubai's desire to push the limits of what is conceivable.

The expression "From Sand to High rises" epitomizes the division that characterizes Dubai's scene. The very desert that was once viewed as an obstruction turned into the wellspring of motivation for structural resourcefulness. The glass exteriors of the high rises mirror the sparkling sands that lay underneath them, making a harmonious connection between the indigenous habitat and human accomplishment. Dubai's horizon, interspersed by modern high rises, is a visual representation for the city's excursion - a demonstration of the change from humble beginnings to worldwide distinction.

The daringness of Dubai's engineering accomplishments is matched exclusively by the city's obligation to supportability. As the world wrestles with natural difficulties, Dubai has embraced eco-accommodating practices in its metropolitan turn of events. The Dubai Reasonable City, a spearheading project, sets new norms for naturally cognizant living. The juxtaposition of state of the art engineering with a pledge to economical practices shows Dubai's purpose to construct a city that goes after the skies as well as proceeds with caution on the Earth.

Past the actual change of the scene, "From Sand to High rises" exemplifies the advancement of Dubai's financial scene. The city, when dependent on oil incomes, decisively differentiated its economy to diminish reliance on a solitary product. The formation of free zones, business-accommodating strategies, and interests in innovation and the travel industry changed Dubai into a worldwide monetary force to be reckoned with.

The Jebel Ali Free Zone, laid out in 1985, pulled in worldwide companies and business people, encouraging a business climate that added to Dubai's financial success. The city's obligation to advancement and business is apparent in the foundation of Dubai Web City and Dubai Media City, which have become center points for innovation and media organizations. Dubai's monetary broadening isn't simply a system; it is an impression of the city's versatility and premonition.

The expression "From Sand to High rises" additionally typifies the social change of Dubai. The city's quick development pulled in a different populace from around the world. Ostracizes, drawn by the commitment of chances and a top notch of life, turned into a vital piece of Dubai's social texture. The multiculturalism that characterizes the city today is a demonstration of its transparency and inclusivity.

Dubai's obligation to protecting its social legacy in the midst of quick modernization is clear in the conservation of authentic destinations, for example, Al Fahidi Stronghold, which houses the Dubai Exhibition hall. The juxtaposition of the old and the new is a conscious work to keep an association with the past while embracing what's to come. Dubai's social story isn't a setback from progress yet a unique power that enhances the city's character.

The expression "From Sand to High rises" isn't simply an ordered record of Dubai's turn of events; a story catches the substance of the city's soul. It addresses the versatility of a local area that flourished in testing conditions, the premonition of pioneers who hoped against hope into the great beyond, and the development that transformed dry scenes into a material for engineering splendor.

As Dubai keeps on going after new levels, the tale of "From Sand to High rises" stays a living demonstration of the city's capacity to ceaselessly rehash itself. The excursion isn't one of conclusiveness however a continuous adventure of development, manageability, and inclusivity. From the grains of sand that once characterized its scene, Dubai has ascended to turn into a worldwide symbol, and the expression fills in as an update that the city's direction isn't restricted by the ground underneath however moved by the limitless yearnings that stretch towards the sky.

1.1 The transformative era of oil discovery and economic boom.

The groundbreaking time of oil revelation in Dubai denotes a vital part in the city's set of experiences, impelling it from an unobtrusive fishing and exchanging town to a worldwide financial force to be reckoned with. The revelation of oil in the Bedouin Landmass during the twentieth century introduced a time of exceptional change, reshaping the financial scene of Dubai as well as its cultural construction, metropolitan turn of events, and worldwide standing. This time of period of prosperity, filled by oil riches, set up for the city's brilliant ascent and established the groundwork for the aggressive activities and stupendous goals that characterize Dubai today.

The mid-twentieth century unfolded with the chance disclosure of oil in the Middle Eastern Promontory, a district that had for quite some time been known for its immense deserts and roaming Bedouin clans. In Dubai, oil was struck in the Fateh oil field in 1966, denoting the start of an extraordinary time. The dark gold underneath the sands carried with it the commitment of thriving, yet the visionary heads of Dubai comprehended that the way to practical development required key preparation and enhancement.

In charge of this extraordinary period was Sheik Rashid canister Saeed Al Maktoum, who expected administration in 1958. Sheik Rashid's premonition and assurance would demonstrate instrumental in controlling Dubai toward a future that stretched out past the limited assets of oil. Perceiving the requirement for monetary broadening, he started a progression of visionary tasks that laid the preparation for Dubai's development as a worldwide financial center point.

The income created from oil sends out gave the monetary means to put resources into foundation projects that would frame the foundation of Dubai's financial turn of events. One of the main undertakings during this period was the development of Port Rashid in 1972. This profound water port worked with oceanic exchange as well as situated Dubai as an imperative player in the worldwide transportation industry. The essential area of the port permitted Dubai to associate with worldwide business sectors, cultivating financial development and establishing the groundwork for the city's rise on the worldwide stage.

The financial expansion powered by oil incomes empowered Dubai to set out on aggressive metropolitan advancement projects that would reclassify its horizon. The income from oil sends out was decisively reinvested into changing the city's foundation, making a cutting edge and cosmopolitan city. The aggressive improvement plans mirrored the initiative's obligation to transforming Dubai into a city that could contend on the worldwide stage.

During this period, Dubai additionally saw the foundation of the Jebel Ali Free Zone in 1985. This business-accommodating territory expected to draw in global enterprises and business people by offering charge impetuses and smoothed out business processes.

The progress of the free zone additionally energized monetary broadening, transforming Dubai into a territorial business center point and drawing in global ventures that added to the city's financial flexibility.

The extraordinary period of oil revelation in Dubai reshaped the city monetarily as well as had significant cultural ramifications. The unexpected convergence of oil abundance achieved a segment shift as the populace expanded, driven by both regular development and a deluge of exiles looking for work open doors. The multiculturalism that portrays Dubai today started to come to fruition during this period as individuals from different foundations and ethnicities showed up in quest for the city's monetary commitment.

The cultural changes were not restricted to socioeconomics; they stretched out to the way of life and desires of Dubai's inhabitants. The recently discovered abundance considered the advancement of current conveniences and framework that raised the personal satisfaction in the city. As Dubai changed from a humble town to a prospering city, the horizon started to change, mirroring the city's freshly discovered opulence and worldwide desires.

The structural scene of Dubai went through an extreme change during the period of oil disclosure and financial expansion. The income from oil sends out worked with the development of present day foundation and famous milestones that would come to characterize Dubai's personality. One such milestone, the Burj Al Middle Easterner, opened its entryways in 1999, remaining as a demonstration of Dubai's obligation to building greatness and extravagance. The Burj Al Middle Easterner's sail-molded outline against the scenery of the Bedouin Bay turned into an image of lavishness and established the vibe for the city's future building tries.

The development of the Burj Al Bedouin was an introduction to a significantly more aggressive venture — the Burj Khalifa. Finished in 2010, the Burj Khalifa remains as the world's tallest structure, puncturing the sky at a level that appeared to be unbelievable only years and years sooner. The development of these famous designs re-imagined Dubai's horizon as well as flagged the city's availability to push the limits of what was viewed as conceivable.

Dubai's horizon, when portrayed by low-ascent structures and customary design, changed into a stunning presentation of innovation. High rises like the Emirates Pinnacles and the Dubai World Exchange Place arose as images of monetary ability, while the Dubai Marina and Jumeirah Ocean side Homes exhibited the city's obligation to making energetic metropolitan networks. Each construction that rose from the sands of Dubai during this period addressed a demonstration of the city's desire and its rise as a worldwide community for exchange, money, and the travel industry.

The financial expansion likewise achieved a change in Dubai's monetary concentration. While oil stayed a critical supporter of the city's riches, vital endeavors were made to enhance the economy and diminish reliance on a solitary product.

Dubai's chiefs perceived the need to situate the city as a worldwide business and the travel industry center, and the income created from oil was decisively put resources into areas like money, innovation, and land.

The foundation of free zones, for example, Dubai Web City and Dubai Media City, pulled in innovation and media organizations, adding to the city's standing as a center point for development and imagination. The Dubai Worldwide Monetary Center (DIFC), initiated in 2004, further fortified Dubai's situation as a worldwide monetary focus, drawing in global banks and monetary organizations.

The travel industry turned into a critical concentration during the time of financial expansion, as Dubai tried to broaden its income streams. The development of notable inns, diversion edifices, and shopping centers changed Dubai into a worldwide the travel industry objective. The Dubai Shopping center, one of the world's biggest shopping and diversion objections, opened its entryways in 2008, turning into an image of the city's obligation to offering unmatched encounters.

The period of oil revelation and financial expansion reshaped Dubai's actual scene as well as added to a social renaissance. The multiculturalism that came about because of the inundation of exiles and the city's worldwide desires prompted a mixing of customs, dialects, and cooking styles. Dubai's obligation to saving its social legacy in the midst of quick modernization is clear in drives, for example, the Dubai Drama, which has a scope of social exhibitions, and the Alserkal Road, a contemporary expressions center point.

1.2 The visionary leadership that propelled Dubai into a global city.

The Visionary Initiative that Moved Dubai into a Worldwide City

The development of Dubai as a worldwide city is a demonstration of the visionary initiative that directed the city through remarkable change and moved it onto the world stage. Behind the sparkling horizon, inventive ventures, and financial enhancement lies a story of vital premonition, nervy desire, and a promise to greatness. The visionary heads of Dubai, especially individuals from the Al Maktoum family, assumed an essential part in forming the fate of the city, diverting it from an unassuming fishing and exchanging town into a worldwide symbol of progress and development.

One of the focal figures in Dubai's groundbreaking process was Sheik Rashid canister Saeed Al Maktoum, who expected administration in 1958. Sheik Rashid's residency denoted a basic period in Dubai's set of experiences, corresponding with the disclosure of oil in the Bedouin Landmass. Rather than surrendering to the charm of quick riches, Sheik Rashid exhibited remarkable foreknowledge by imagining a future past oil reliance. He comprehended that the limited idea of oil assets expected an essential way to deal with guarantee supported flourishing.

Sheik Rashid's authority was described by a progression of strong and ground breaking drives that established the groundwork for Dubai's change. One of the trademark projects during his time was the development of Port Rashid in 1972. This profound water port improved Dubai's oceanic capacities as well as situated the city as a central participant in the worldwide delivery industry. The essential area of the port worked with productive exchange and set up for Dubai's monetary enhancement.

Perceiving the significance of monetary expansion, Sheik Rashid's vision reached out to the production of free zones, which offered a helpful climate for global organizations to flourish. The foundation of the Jebel Ali Free Zone in 1985 was an essential move that pulled in worldwide partnerships and business people, laying the basis for Dubai's rise as a worldwide business and planned operations center point. The free zones cultivated monetary development as well as added to the multiculturalism that characterizes Dubai today.

Sheik Rashid's administration was not restricted to monetary drives; it additionally reached out to metropolitan turn of events. The city's horizon started to change under his supervision, with an emphasis on present day framework and conveniences that raised the personal satisfaction for occupants. The development of Dubai World Exchange Community 1979, a notable image of the city's monetary desires, exemplified Sheik Rashid's obligation to situating Dubai as a worldwide business objective.

The groundbreaking vision set out by Sheik Rashid was conveyed forward by his child, Sheik Mohammed container Rashid Al Maktoum, who accepted administration in 2006. Sheik Mohammed's initiative style is portrayed by a persevering quest for greatness, development, and a promise to pushing the limits of probability. Under his direction, Dubai entered another period of dynamic turn of events, set apart by aggressive tasks and an enhancement of the city's economy.

Quite possibly of the most significant venture under Sheik Mohammed's administration is the Burj Khalifa, finished in 2010. Taking off to exceptional levels, the Burj Khalifa remains as the world's tallest structure, a demonstration of Dubai's obligation to engineering development and worldwide noticeable quality. The Burj Khalifa, with its advanced plan and state of the art innovation, represents the city's rising as well as its assurance to feature greatness on the world stage.

The Burj Khalifa is important for a more extensive vision embodied in Sheik Mohammed's drive known as "Vision 2021." This visionary guide frames vital objectives for Dubai, enveloping financial expansion, social turn of events, and the foundation of Dubai as a worldwide center for different businesses. Vision 2021 reflects Sheik Mohammed's obligation to making a feasible and comprehensive future for Dubai, with an accentuation on development, information, and bliss.

The financial enhancement methodologies carried out under Sheik Mohammed's administration stretch out to areas like the travel industry, innovation, and money. The development of milestone projects, like the Palm Jumeirah and The World, displayed Dubai's designing ability and changed the city into a worldwide the travel industry objective. The Dubai Shopping center, one of the world's biggest shopping and diversion edifices, turned into a center point for retail, recreation, and social encounters.

The Dubai Global Monetary Center (DIFC), laid out in 2004, is one more illustration of Sheik Mohammed's obligation to expanding the city's economy. As a monetary free zone, DIFC draws in worldwide banks, monetary organizations, and organizations, adding to Dubai's status as a worldwide monetary center. Sheik Mohammed's vision for an enhanced and tough economy is obvious in the outcome of these drives, situating Dubai as a city that isn't exclusively reliant upon oil income.

Sheik Mohammed's initiative is portrayed by an emphasis on development and innovative headway. The foundation of free zones, for example, Dubai Web City and Dubai Media City pulled in innovation and media organizations, encouraging a climate of imagination and business venture. The Shrewd Dubai drive, sent off in 2013, means to change Dubai into a brilliant city by utilizing innovation to improve effectiveness, maintainability, and personal satisfaction.

The obligation to development is likewise reflected in the Dubai Future Establishment and the Dubai Future Gas pedals program, which try to situate Dubai as a worldwide advancement center point. These drives highlight Sheik Mohammed's acknowledgment of the significance of remaining at the cutting edge of mechanical progressions and cultivating a climate where advancement flourishes.

Past monetary and innovative drives, Sheik Mohammed has shown a promise to social turn of events and inclusivity. The "My People group... A City for Everybody" drive endeavors to make a strong and comprehensive society where occupants of different foundations feel a feeling of having a place. The accentuation on joy and prosperity as fundamental parts of Dubai's advancement exhibits Sheik Mohammed's comprehensive way to deal with administration.

The multiculturalism that characterizes Dubai is a demonstration of the progress of Sheik Mohammed's vision for a comprehensive and different society. The city's ostracize populace, drawn from north of 200 identities, adds to an energetic social embroidery. The social drives, like the Dubai Show and the Emirates Carrier Celebration of Writing, reflect Sheik Mohammed's obligation to supporting human expression and protecting the city's social legacy.

The authority of Sheik Mohammed has not exclusively been instrumental in molding Dubai's present yet in addition in diagramming a course for its future.

The Exhibition 2020 Dubai, initially made arrangements for 2020 however deferred to 2021 because of the worldwide pandemic, is an indication of Sheik Mohammed's vision for Dubai as a worldwide objective for development and coordinated effort. The exhibition is supposed to grandstand state of the art advancements, encourage global collaboration, and further lift Dubai's status on the world stage.

1.3 The iconic architectural marvels that define the city's skyline.

The Famous Structural Wonders that Characterize Dubai's Horizon

Dubai's horizon remains as a demonstration of the city's daring desire and unfaltering obligation to structural greatness. From the once-unobtrusive fishing and exchanging town along the Bedouin Inlet, Dubai has changed into a worldwide city decorated with notable designs that puncture the sky and enamor the world's creative mind. The city's design wonders are not just designs; they are images of development, extravagance, and the unyielding soul that has pushed Dubai onto the worldwide stage.

At the front of Dubai's compositional wonders is the Burj Khalifa, a notable image of the city's desire to arrive at new levels — straightforwardly. Finished in 2010, the Burj Khalifa remains as the world's tallest structure, taking off to a level of 828 meters (2,717 feet). The plan of the Burj Khalifa is a magnum opus of current design, highlighting a smooth, tightening structure that comes full circle in a needle-like tower. The outside of the pinnacle is enhanced with a shining glass drapery wall that mirrors the changing shades of the sky, making a visual display.

The Burj Khalifa isn't simply a transcending structure; an accomplishment of designing and configuration pushed the limits of what was considered conceivable. The development of the Burj Khalifa involved imaginative designing answers for address difficulties, for example, wind powers, temperature differentials, and establishment dependability. The outcome is a structure that stands as a designing wonder as well as fills in as an image of Dubai's assurance to reclassify the restrictions of compositional accomplishment.

As guests rise the Burj Khalifa, they are blessed to receive all encompassing perspectives on Dubai and then some. The perception decks on the upper floors give a stunning vantage point, offering vistas that stretch across the city, the Bedouin Inlet, and the encompassing desert. The Burj Khalifa, with its mix of level, plan, and usefulness, has turned into a notorious portrayal of Dubai's horizon, a signal that draws guests and admirers from around the world.

Neighboring the Burj Khalifa lies another structural marvel that graces Dubai's scene — the Dubai Shopping center. While not a particular construction in the customary sense, the Dubai Shopping center is a huge complex that coordinates shopping, diversion, and recreation in a consistent combination of plan and usefulness. Opened in 2008, the Dubai Shopping center is one of the biggest shopping and diversion objections worldwide, traversing more than 12 million square feet.

The Dubai Shopping center isn't simply a retail space; an experiential location mirrors Dubai's obligation to giving unrivaled extravagance and diversion. The shopping center is home to more than 1,300 shops, highlighting a blend of worldwide extravagance brands and neighborhood stores. Past shopping, the Dubai Shopping center offers a different cluster of attractions, including a very large ice arena, an indoor cascade, an aquarium highlighting north of 33,000 marine creatures, and, surprisingly, an indoor amusement park — KidZania.

One of the most famous highlights of the Dubai Shopping center is its entry, which faces the Burj Khalifa and highlights the entrancing Dubai Wellspring. This arranged wellspring, set against the background of the Burj Khalifa, turns into a stupendous presentation of light, water, and music in the nights, enrapturing guests and occupants the same. The Dubai Shopping center, with its combination of extravagance retail, amusement, and compositional loftiness, epitomizes Dubai's obligation to making spaces that rise above customary definitions and proposition vivid encounters.

Settled off the shore of Dubai is the Palm Jumeirah, a counterfeit archipelago that is a wonder of both designing and plan. Formed like a palm tree, the Palm Jumeirah is a demonstration of Dubai's capacity to change its waterfront scene and make islands with a particular reason. The Palm Jumeirah, finished in 2009, highlights a blend of private, business, and cordiality improvements, making it quite possibly of the most pursued address in Dubai.

The Palm Jumeirah isn't simply a private and business center point; it is a notable milestone noticeable from space and a demonstration of human resourcefulness. The development of the Palm Jumeirah involved broad land recovery and the production of a multifaceted organization of sea walls and bow molded fronds. The outcome is a palm-molded island that reaches out into the Bedouin Inlet, with extravagance homes, inns, and resorts covering its fronds and bows.

Perhaps of the most conspicuous construction on the Palm Jumeirah is the Atlantis, The Palm — a five-star inn and resort that stands as an image of extravagance and plushness. The Atlantis highlights interesting building components, including a scaffold suite that traverses the hotel's two pinnacles and offers stunning perspectives on the city and the Middle Eastern Inlet. The Palm Jumeirah, with its creative plan and vital situating, has turned into a famous component of Dubai's horizon, mirroring the city's capacity to reshape nature in quest for amazing dreams.

Relatively close to the Palm Jumeirah is another design work of art that graces the shoreline — the Burj Al Bedouin. Finished in 1999, the Burj Al Middle Easterner isn't only an inn; it is an image of extravagance, selectiveness, and design development. Formed like the sail of a dhow, a conventional Middle Eastern cruising vessel, the Burj Al Bedouin remains on its own counterfeit island and is associated with the central area by an interstate.

The Burj Al Bedouin's plan is a combination of conventional Middle Eastern components and contemporary extravagance. The utilization of intelligent materials, for example, Teflon-covered fiberglass, gives the structure a particular appearance that changes tints with the daylight. The inside of the Burj Al Middle Easterner is similarly extravagant, including sumptuous suites, eateries with all encompassing perspectives, and a huge chamber with a flowing cascade. The Burj Al Middle Easterner isn't just an inn; it is an image of Dubai's obligation to offering the greatest possible level of in extravagance and neighborliness.

Dubai's horizon is additionally accentuated by the structural miracles that structure the Dubai Marina. This counterfeit trench city, worked along a two-mile stretch of the Bedouin Inlet coastline, is a demonstration of Dubai's capacity to make metropolitan scenes that orchestrate with the regular habitat. The Dubai Marina, finished in 2003, highlights a blend of private and business towers, waterfront promenades, and a different cluster of eating and diversion choices.

The highlight of the Dubai Marina is the Cayan Pinnacle, a compositional wonder known for its contorting shape. The Cayan Pinnacle, finished in 2013, is a private high rise that turns 90 degrees as it climbs, making a dynamic and outwardly striking outline. This imaginative plan not just upgrades the tasteful allure of the pinnacle yet in addition augments the all encompassing perspectives on the encompassing region.

The Dubai Marina is supplemented by the Jumeirah Ocean side Home (JBR), a clamoring waterfront local area that highlights private pinnacles, retail outlets, and an energetic ocean front promenade. The juxtaposition of current engineering against the setting of the Middle Eastern Inlet causes a beautiful situation that catches the quintessence of Dubai's cosmopolitan way of life.

Another milestone that embellishes Dubai's horizon is the Dubai Casing, a demonstration of the city's respect for its past and its hug of innovation. Finished in 2018, the Dubai Edge is a transcending rectangular construction that casings perspectives on the old and new Dubai. The plan represents a scaffold between the city's legacy and its future, with one side contribution perspectives on the noteworthy neighborhoods of Deira and Bramble Dubai, and the opposite side displaying the cutting edge horizon with milestones like the Burj Khalifa.

The Dubai Edge isn't just a perception point; a design welcomes reflection on Dubai's excursion from an unobtrusive town to a worldwide city. The straightforward glass span at the highest point of the edge offers guests an extraordinary viewpoint as they stroll between the different sides, representing the city's development and the interconnectedness of its at various times.

Dubai's obligation to pushing compositional limits is exemplified by progressing and arranged projects that keep on reclassifying the city's horizon. The Dubai Spring Pinnacle, under development starting around the last information update in 2022, is ready to outperform the Burj Khalifa in level upon finishing. The pinnacle's plan is motivated by the lily bloom and epitomizes Dubai's devotion to making structures that overwhelm the horizon as well as stretch the boundaries of design and designing development.

Chapter 2

"Cultural Kaleidoscope"

Social Kaleidoscope: Dubai's Rich Embroidery of Variety

Dubai, a city that rose up out of the bone-dry sands of the Bedouin Promontory, isn't just a worldwide monetary center point and engineering wonder yet in addition an energetic mosaic of societies. The expression "Social Kaleidoscope" embodies the rich embroidery of variety that characterizes Dubai's social texture. From its unassuming starting points as a little fishing and exchanging town to its ongoing status as a worldwide city, Dubai has invited individuals from around the world, making an exceptional mix of customs, dialects, and customs that add to the city's cosmopolitan character.

The multiculturalism that describes Dubai today is a consequence of many years of financial development, vital preparation, and a receptiveness to the worldwide local area. The city's initiative, perceiving the significance of an assorted and comprehensive society, has encouraged a climate where individuals from various foundations can coincide and add to the city's prosperity.

Dubai's excursion into multiculturalism started decisively with the revelation of oil during the twentieth 100 years. The deluge of ostracizes looking for work potential open doors assumed a critical part in molding the city's segment scene. As the city changed from a local general store into a worldwide monetary force to be reckoned with, the populace expanded with people from different corners of the globe.

Today, Dubai is home to a tremendous exile populace that addresses more than 200 identities. The variety is clear in each feature of life, from the dialects expressed in the city to the variety of foods accessible in the city's eateries. This mixture of societies has turned into a characterizing component of Dubai's personality, improving the city's social elements and adding to its worldwide allure.

One of the critical supporters of Dubai's social kaleidoscope is the presence of various exile networks that have secured themselves inside the city. These people group frequently structure lively neighborhoods where inhabitants praise their social practices, share customs, and make a feeling of usual hangout spot. Little India, for instance, is a clamoring neighborhood where the sights, sounds, and kinds of India wake up. Essentially, regions like Al Rigga and Al Satwa are known for their lively blend of societies, offering a brief look into the different foundations of their occupants.

The multiculturalism in Dubai isn't restricted to explicit areas yet penetrates each part of day to day existence. It is obvious in the work environment, where associates from various regions of the planet team up on undertakings and offer thoughts. It is noticeable in the instructive establishments, where understudies from different foundations learn next to each other, encouraging a worldwide viewpoint since the beginning. The social blending is definitely not a simple conjunction; a unique trade shapes the city's personality and adds to a feeling of solidarity in variety.

Dubai's obligation to social variety is reflected in its commitment to safeguarding and advancing the legacy of its occupant networks. The city has various social celebrations and occasions that exhibit the practices, music, dance, and cooking of different identities. The yearly Dubai Shopping Celebration, for example, changes the city into a social spectacle, with occasions and exhibitions that feature the variety of the worldwide local area calling Dubai home.

One of the perfect representations of Dubai's obligation to social protection is the architecturally significant area of Al Fahidi, where the Al Fahidi Post has been changed into the Dubai Gallery. The historical center furnishes guests with a brief look into the city's past, displaying the conventional lifestyle before the period of high rises and cutting edge improvements. The juxtaposition of the old and the new is an intentional work to respect the foundations of the city while embracing what's in store.

Dubai's multiculturalism is additionally reflected in its strict resistance. The city is home to various mosques, houses of worship, sanctuaries, and temples, permitting inhabitants to unreservedly rehearse their confidence. The Jumeirah Mosque, with its dazzling engineering, fills in as an image of Islamic culture and friendliness, offering directed visits to guests, everything being equal, to advance comprehension and enthusiasm for the Islamic confidence.

The social variety stretches out past conventional practices to the domain of expressions and amusement. Dubai has arisen as a worldwide center point for human expression, with drives, for example, Alserkal Road encouraging a flourishing contemporary craftsmanship scene. The Dubai Drama, a design pearl, has different exhibitions going from traditional shows to Broadway shows, taking special care of assorted imaginative preferences.

Social variety is additionally celebrated through writing, with occasions like the Emirates Aircraft Celebration of Writing drawing in famous writers and educated people from around the world. The celebration fills in as a stage for the trading of thoughts and the investigation of various scholarly customs.

The "Social Kaleidoscope" is additionally advanced by Dubai's obligation to development and innovation. The city's authority perceives that embracing variety isn't just an issue of social union yet additionally a competitive edge in a globalized world. Dubai Web City and Dubai Media City, laid out as free zones, have drawn in innovation and media organizations, adding to the city's status as a worldwide place for development and imagination.

The multiculturalism in Dubai isn't without its difficulties, however the city's administration has reliably pursued making a comprehensive society where occupants of different foundations feel a feeling of having a place. Drives like the "My People group... A City for Everybody" program intend to advance social union, underscoring that Dubai is a city where individuals from various different backgrounds can reside, work, and flourish together.

The "Social Kaleidoscope" of Dubai is a story of conjunction, trade, and shared goals. A story started with the union of different societies in quest for monetary open doors and has developed into an agreeable mix of customs, dialects, and customs. Dubai's multiculturalism isn't static; it is dynamic, advancing as time passes as the city keeps on drawing in people from around the world, each adding to the energetic mosaic that is Dubai.

2.1 Exploration of Dubai's diverse cultural landscape.

Investigation of Dubai's Assorted Social Scene

Dubai, a city brought into the world from the immense stretches of desert along the Bedouin Bay, has changed into a worldwide city that stands as a demonstration of the amicable conjunction of different societies.

From its unassuming starting points as a little fishing and exchanging town, Dubai's social scene has developed into a rich embroidery woven with strings from around the world. This investigation digs into the horde features of Dubai's social variety, following its underlying foundations, inspecting the present, and imagining the fate of a city that embraces the world inside its limits.

Verifiable Establishments: An Embroidery Unfurling

Dubai's social process starts with its verifiable establishments as an exchanging and pearl-jumping town. Arranged at a junction of old shipping lanes, Dubai turned into a blend of Middle Eastern, Persian, and Indian impacts. The customary business sectors, or souks, that specked the waterfront were centers of business and social trade, where merchants from different foundations took part in deal and business.

The Al Fahidi Architecturally significant area, previously known as Al Bastakiya, gives a brief look into Dubai's past. The locale safeguards the customary engineering of wind-tower houses, slender paths, and patios, offering guests an unmistakable connection to the city's modest starting points. The Al Fahidi Post, changed into the Dubai Gallery, fills in as a period container, portraying the tale of Dubai's development from an unobtrusive town to a worldwide city.

As the city embraced innovation, it didn't leave its foundations. The verifiable regions stand as a distinct difference to the glimmering high rises that presently characterize Dubai's horizon, filling in as an impactful sign of the city's obligation to saving its legacy in the midst of quick turn of events.

Multicultural Present: A Worldwide Social occasion Point

Dubai's present is portrayed by a multicultural scene that mirrors the city's development into a worldwide center point for business, the travel industry, and development. The revelation of oil during the twentieth century denoted a defining moment, drawing in a flood of ostracizes looking for work open doors. Today, Dubai is home to a different populace addressing north of 200 ethnicities, making a social mosaic that is unrivaled in its extravagance.

The multiculturalism is discernible in each feature of day to day existence. The working environment is a mixture where experts from different foundations team up, carrying a worldwide point of view to business tries. The city's instructive foundations are microcosms of the world, encouraging a climate where understudies from different social foundations learn next to each other, planning for a globalized future.

Neighborhoods like Al Rigga, Al Satwa, and Little India act as social center points, where the sights, sounds, and kinds of various districts wake up. These regions are not simply private quarters; they are dynamic networks that celebrate variety, making spaces where occupants track down commonality and brotherhood amidst a worldwide city.

Dubai's obligation to social variety is exemplified by its devotion to safeguarding and advancing the legacy of its occupant networks. The city has various social celebrations and occasions that feature the customs, music, dance, and food of different identities. The yearly Dubai Shopping Celebration, for example, changes the city into a social party, with occasions and exhibitions that feature the variety of the worldwide local area calling Dubai home.

Strict resilience is a foundation of Dubai's social scene. The city is home to mosques, places of worship, sanctuaries, and temples, permitting occupants to unreservedly rehearse their confidence. This soul of inclusivity is an impression of Dubai's obligation to giving an inviting climate to individuals, everything being equal.

Culinary variety is one more sign of Dubai's multicultural present. The city's culinary scene is a worldwide range, offering a gastronomic excursion that traverses landmasses. From customary Emirati dishes to colorful worldwide cooking styles, Dubai's cafés take care of assorted preferences, mirroring the shifted inclinations of its cosmopolitan populace.

Social protection and advancement are not bound to explicit drives however are woven into the texture of Dubai's turn of events. The Dubai Drama, a cutting edge building diamond, has various exhibitions that range social sorts, from old style shows to Broadway shows. The city's obligation to human expressions is further obvious in drives like Alserkal Road, a contemporary expressions center point that gives a stage to neighborhood and worldwide craftsmen to grandstand their work.

Visionary Future: Supporting Social Concordance

Dubai's obligation to social variety is certainly not a static achievement yet a continuous exertion that shapes the city's direction into what's in store. The initiative of Dubai imagines a city that keeps on being a worldwide blend, where individuals from various foundations flourish and add to the aggregate advancement of the local area.

One of the key drives that support Dubai's vision for what's in store is the "My People group... A City for Everybody" program. This program underscores the significance of social attachment and inclusivity, advancing a feeling of having a place for inhabitants from different foundations. By cultivating a culture of understanding and acknowledgment, Dubai plans to make a general public where individuals of all identities and societies feel at ease.

The Exhibition 2020 Dubai, initially made arrangements for 2020 however deferred to 2021 because of the worldwide pandemic, is a demonstration of Dubai's obligation to worldwide coordinated effort and social trade. The exhibition is intended to be a stage where countries meet up to grandstand their developments, societies, and goals. It is a sign of Dubai's job as a worldwide city that flourishes with variety and tries to fabricate scaffolds of understanding among countries.

Dubai's initiative perceives that supporting social concordance requires an all encompassing methodology that goes past strategies and projects. The city's obligation to development and innovation lines up with its vision for a future where variety isn't simply endured however celebrated. Drives like the Dubai Future Establishment and the Dubai Future Gas pedals program position Dubai as a worldwide development center, embracing mechanical progressions and encouraging a climate where inventiveness knows no limits.

The continuous development of the Dubai Stream Pinnacle, expected to outperform the Burj Khalifa in level upon finish, represents Dubai's desire to arrive at new levels while keeping an association with its foundations. The pinnacle's plan is roused by the lily bloom, exhibiting a reconciliation of nature and innovation. This venture epitomizes Dubai's obligation to pushing structural and designing limits while embracing an economical and socially cognizant future.

2.2 Celebration of the city's tolerance and inclusivity.

Festivity of the City's Resistance and Inclusivity

Dubai, frequently alluded to as the "City of Gold," has amassed abundance through its financial ability as well as developed a standing for being a stronghold of resistance and inclusivity. In a world frequently defaced by divisions, Dubai stands apart as a reference point of solidarity, where individuals from different foundations coincide agreeably. The festival of the city's resilience and inclusivity is a story that rises above simple manner of speaking; it is implanted in the city's ethos, forming strategies, social drives, and the day to day routines of its occupants.

A Social Blend:

At the core of Dubai's festival of resilience is its status as a genuine social mixture. The city's segment cosmetics is a kaleidoscope of identities, nationalities, and religions.

Individuals from more than 200 nations have made Dubai their home, making a social texture that is unpredictably woven with strings from each edge of the globe.

The resilience in Dubai is definitely not a latent conjunction yet a functioning festival of variety. The city's initiative has embraced the possibility that an amicable society is one that appreciates and regards the distinctions among its occupants. This responsibility is reflected in strategies that advance inclusivity, like the issuance of long haul visas to occupants, regardless of their identity.

The neighborhoods of Dubai are microcosms of this social variety. From the notable regions like Al Fahidi, where the breeze tower houses murmur stories of the past, to the clamoring areas like Al Rigga and Al Satwa, where the energy of various societies wakes up, Dubai's roads are an impression of the world's heap customs.

Strict Concordance:

Dubai's festival of resistance stretches out to strict inclusivity. The city is home to mosques, chapels, sanctuaries, and temples, making an amicable conjunction of different strict practices. The Jumeirah Mosque, with its shocking design, remains as an image of Islamic culture and neighborliness. It makes its ways for guests, everything being equal, offering directed visits to encourage understanding and enthusiasm for the Islamic confidence.

The St. Mary's Catholic Church, the Shiva and Krishna Mandir, and the Gurudwara Dubai are demonstration of the city's obligation to giving spaces to strict practices past Islam. This strict variety isn't restricted to spots of love; it is woven into the texture of day to day existence, where people from various religions meet up in the soul of shared regard and understanding.

The Time of Resilience, pronounced by the UAE government in 2019, further highlighted Dubai's obligation to advancing discourse among various religions and societies. The year saw drives and occasions that accentuated the upsides of resilience and inclusivity, cultivating a climate where people could take part in open discussions about their convictions.

Legitimate System of Resistance:

Dubai's festival of resilience isn't just a social peculiarity; it is likewise cherished in the city's legitimate system. The UAE's constitution ensures opportunity of religion and conviction, accentuating the standards of resilience and acknowledgment. The overall set of laws maintains the freedoms of people to rehearse their confidence and shields them from segregation in view of religion or ethnicity.

The foundation of the UAE's Service of Resistance in 2016 denoted a huge move toward standardizing the upsides of resilience. The service assumes a pivotal part in advancing these qualities both locally and globally. Its drives incorporate instructive projects, widespread developments, and associations with different associations to cultivate an ethos of resistance and inclusivity.

Instructive Drives:

A basic part of Dubai's festival of resistance is its attention on training. The city perceives that developing resistance starts with sustaining youthful personalities to see the value in variety and embrace inclusivity. Dubai's instructive establishments assume an essential part in imparting these qualities in the future.

Schools in Dubai take on educational programs that underline social variety, worldwide mindfulness, and the significance of resistance. Understudies are presented to a rich embroidery of societies, permitting them to grasp, regard, and celebrate contrasts. Instructive projects additionally advance discourse among understudies from different foundations, encouraging a climate where companionships and shared understanding can prosper.

Colleges in Dubai further add to the festival of resilience by drawing in understudies from around the world. The multicultural climate of these foundations is a microcosm of Dubai's more extensive society, where understudies from different foundations team up on projects, trade thoughts, and structure enduring associations that reach out past the study hall.

Social Celebrations and Occasions:

Dubai's obligation to commending resilience is clear in its energetic schedule of social celebrations and occasions. These social occasions give stages to individuals from various foundations to feature their customs, share their accounts, and take part in significant discussions.

The yearly Dubai Shopping Celebration, for instance, goes past being a retail event. It changes the city into a social fair, with occasions that feature the variety of the worldwide local area calling Dubai home. Live events, workmanship presentations, and food celebrations add to the social embroidered artwork of the city, encouraging a climate where occupants and guests the same can delight in the lavishness of various customs.

The Dubai Show, a structural wonder, has exhibitions that length social classifications, offering a phase for craftsmen from different regions of the planet. The Emirates Carrier Celebration of Writing unites abstract personalities from different foundations, encouraging a trade of thoughts and viewpoints.

Inclusivity in the Working environment:

Dubai's festival of resistance reaches out to the working environment, where people from various identities and societies team up in quest for shared objectives. The city's status as a worldwide business center draws in experts from around the world, establishing a workplace that blossoms with variety.

Organizations in Dubai perceive the worth of a multicultural labor force and effectively advance inclusivity in their strategies and practices. Racial awareness coaching programs, social mindfulness drives, and representative asset bunches add to cultivating an air where each individual feels esteemed and regarded.

Vision for What's in store:

Dubai's festival of resilience is definitely not a static accomplishment; a continuous responsibility shapes the city's vision for what's to come. The initiative of Dubai imagines a future where resilience isn't simply an uprightness yet a lifestyle. The city's drives, for example, the Dubai Future Establishment and the Dubai Future Gas pedals program, position Dubai as a worldwide development center point, embracing innovative headways while keeping a guarantee to inclusivity.

The Exhibition 2020 Dubai, delayed to 2021 because of the worldwide pandemic, is a sign of Dubai's obligation to worldwide joint effort and social trade. The exhibition is intended to be a stage where countries meet up to grandstand their developments, societies, and desires. It is a chance for Dubai to additionally support job as a city blossoms with variety and tries to fabricate extensions of understanding among countries.

2.3 The role of cultural institutions, festivals, and events in shaping Dubai's identity.

The Job of Social Establishments, Celebrations, and Occasions in Forming Dubai's Personality

Dubai, a city that has ascended from the desert to turn into a worldwide city, isn't simply characterized by its transcending high rises and monetary ability; it is likewise molded by its lively social scene. Social establishments, celebrations, and occasions assume a critical part in winding around the texture of Dubai's personality, giving spaces to imaginative articulation, encouraging a feeling of local area, and adding to the city's story as a center point of imagination and development.

Social Foundations as Mainstays of Personality:

Social foundations in Dubai act as support points that anchor the city's personality, spanning the past with the present and molding what's to come. One such establishment is the Dubai Gallery, situated in the Al Fahidi Architecturally significant area. Housed in the Al Fahidi Post, the gallery gives an excursion through time, offering bits of knowledge into Dubai's unassuming starting points as a fishing town and its change into a worldwide city.

The Dubai Exhibition hall isn't only a store of relics; it is a living demonstration of the city's obligation to safeguarding its legacy in the midst of fast modernization. The shows, going from customary homes to presentations of old oceanic exchange, make a story that interfaces inhabitants and guests the same with the foundations of Dubai. The historical center fills in as an instructive center, encouraging an appreciation for the rich history that supports the city's contemporary character.

Notwithstanding the Dubai Gallery, establishments like the Etihad Exhibition hall and the Alserkal Road expressions area add to Dubai's social scene. The Etihad Gallery, introduced in 2017, centers around the historical backdrop of the Unified Middle Easterner Emirates, giving a far reaching outline of the occasions that prompted the nation's development. Alserkal Road, then again, is a contemporary expressions space that has displays, studios, and inventive organizations, situating Dubai as a center point for current creative articulation.

The Dubai Drama, another famous social foundation, addresses a union of custom and innovation. Its engineering honors the conventional dhow sails while its insides have a different cluster of exhibitions, going from old style dramas to contemporary shows. The Dubai Drama fills in as an image of the city's obligation to encouraging a social renaissance that embraces the two legacy and the worldwide impacts shape its personality.

Celebrations: Observing Variety and Solidarity:

Dubai's social character is likewise celebrated through a bunch of celebrations that unite occupants and guests in a common festival of variety and solidarity. One of the most unmistakable occasions is the Dubai Shopping Celebration (DSF), a yearly event that changes the city into a mixture of societies and a worldwide shopping objective. Past the retail perspective, DSF highlights social exhibitions, music shows, and culinary occasions that feature the city's cosmopolitan nature.

The yearly Emirates Carrier Celebration of Writing is one more demonstration of Dubai's obligation to cultivating an affection for writing and scholarly talk. The celebration draws in prestigious creators, writers, and erudite people from around the world, making a stage for the trading of thoughts and the festival of scholarly variety. Book devotees, the two occupants and global guests, take part in a progression of meetings, studios, and conversations that add to Dubai's way of life as a middle for scholarly and social commitment.

Dubai's obligation to inclusivity and understanding is highlighted by the recognition of the Extended period of Resilience in 2019. The year saw a large number of occasions and drives pointed toward advancing resilience and social trade. The Dubai Resilience Culmination, held during the year, united thought pioneers, policymakers, and specialists to examine techniques for cultivating a more open minded and comprehensive society. This drive commended the city's obligation to resistance as well as situated Dubai as a worldwide forerunner in advancing these qualities.

Creative Articulation and Present day Social Centers:

Dubai's social personality isn't bound to customary types of articulation; it reaches out to the domain of contemporary craftsmanship and advancement. The Alserkal Road expressions region, arranged in the modern Al Quoz region, has arisen as a unique center for contemporary workmanship. Home to various displays, studios, and innovative spaces, Alserkal Road is a sign of Dubai's hug of current creative articulation.

The area has ordinary craftsmanship displays, establishments, and far-reaching developments that draw in both nearby and global specialists. It gives a stage to inventive personalities to exhibit their work, adding to the city's story as a worldwide place for contemporary craftsmanship. The combination of conventional Emirati impacts with cutting edge imaginative articulations mirrors Dubai's dynamic way of life as a city that values development and social variety.

Dubai Configuration Region (d3) is one more contemporary social center that exhibits the convergence of configuration, design, and imagination. With its cutting edge framework and an emphasis on sustaining arising ability, d3 has turned into a core for the plan local area. Yearly occasions like Dubai Plan Week unite originators, designers, and devotees from around the world, adding a cutting edge layer to Dubai's social character.

Social Variety in Culinary Expressions:

Dubai's character is likewise complicatedly associated with its culinary scene, which is a dynamic impression of the city's multicultural texture. The conventional Emirati cooking, with its rich flavors and fragrances, coincides with a plenty of global foods, making a culinary scene that reflects the city's variety.

The Worldwide Town, a yearly occasion that runs from November to April, typifies Dubai's festival of worldwide culinary variety. The occasion highlights structures addressing various nations, each offering a gastronomic excursion through its conventional dishes. It is a blend of flavors, smells, and culinary procedures, epitomizing Dubai's way of life as a city that embraces the world through its sense of taste.

Visionary Undertakings: Pushing Social Limits:

Dubai's obligation to molding its social character reaches out to visionary undertakings that push the limits of imaginative articulation and development. The Dubai Casing, finished in 2018, is a great representation of such a venture. The transcending rectangular construction outlines perspectives on the old and new Dubai, representing a scaffold between the city's legacy and its future. The straightforward glass span at the highest point of the casing gives guests a special viewpoint, welcoming consideration on the city's development.

Progressing projects, for example, the Dubai River Pinnacle and the Exhibition hall Representing things to come, epitomize Dubai's aspiration to reclassify its social scene. The Dubai Brook Pinnacle, set to outperform the Burj Khalifa in level, addresses a union of compositional wonderfulness and natural maintainability. The pinnacle's plan, motivated by the lily bloom, connotes the city's devotion to making structures that rule the horizon as well as add to an economical and socially cognizant future.

The Exhibition hall Representing things to come, a cutting edge project set to open before long, plans to be a stage for development and inventiveness. It imagines a space where state of the art innovations, logical headways, and creative articulations meet, molding Dubai's way of life as a city at the front of progress and social development.

Chapter 3

"Trade and Innovation Hub"

Exchange and Advancement Center point: Dubai's Dynamic Job in World-wide Trade and Imagination

Dubai, the clamoring city that rose up out of the bone-dry scenes of the Bedouin Landmass, has changed into a dynamic focal point of worldwide exchange and development. Its essential area at the junction of East and West, combined with visionary initiative and aggressive framework projects, has pushed Dubai into an exchange and development center point. This investigation dives into the complex features of Dubai's dynamic job, looking at its development from a little exchanging port to a worldwide monetary stalwart that embraces advancement and imagination.

Exchange Roots: The Authentic Establishment

Dubai's excursion as an exchange and development center point is well established in its verifiable beginnings as a little fishing and exchanging town. The essential area along old shipping lanes added to the city's initial monetary exercises, with merchants participating in the trading of products going from pearls to flavors. The customary souks that lined the waterfront were clamoring focuses of business, making way for Dubai's future as an exchanging force to be reckoned with.

The city's rulers, perceiving the capability of exchange, carried out strategies that cultivated an open and business-accommodating climate. The foundation of the Dubai Stream as a deregulation zone in the mid twentieth century laid the basis for the city's development into a worldwide exchanging center. This ground breaking approach pulled in shippers and merchants from around the locale, establishing the groundwork for the monetary thriving that was to come.

Vital Vision: The Job of Administration

Dubai's climb as an exchange and development center can be credited to the visionary initiative that perceived the requirement for expansion and manageable turn of events. Sheik Rashid receptacle Saeed Al Maktoum, the Leader of Dubai from 1958 to 1990, assumed a crucial part in directing the city towards monetary success.

His premonition laid the foundation for aggressive ventures that would change Dubai into a cutting edge city.

One of the milestone choices was the foundation of the Jebel Ali Free Zone in 1985. This deregulation zone, portrayed by its business-accommodating guidelines and cutting edge framework, turned into a magnet for global organizations trying to lay out a presence in the Center East. It denoted an essential move towards broadening the economy and utilizing the capability of worldwide exchange.

The light of initiative was passed to Sheik Mohammed receptacle Rashid Al Maktoum, the VP and Head of the state of the UAE and Leader of Dubai, who proceeded with the tradition of advancement and improvement. Under his direction, Dubai set out on aggressive tasks, including the notorious Burj Khalifa and the Palm Jumeirah. These endeavors improved the city's horizon as well as situated Dubai as an image of innovation and progress.

Free Zones and Monetary Enhancement:

Dubai's prosperity as an exchange and development center is complicatedly connected to the foundation of free zones that give a favorable climate to business development. Free zones, like Jebel Ali, Dubai Web City, and Dubai Media City, offer impetuses like 100 percent unfamiliar possession, charge exceptions, and improved on customs techniques. These drives draw in global companies, new businesses, and business people, encouraging a powerful environment of development and trade.

Dubai Web City, sent off in 1999, centers around data and correspondence innovation. It has turned into a center point for tech organizations, new businesses, and computerized business visionaries, establishing a climate where development flourishes. Likewise, Dubai Media City plays had an essential impact in molding the city's way of life as a local media and diversion center, facilitating worldwide media goliaths and encouraging an imaginative local area.

The broadening of the economy past oil and gas was an essential move to guarantee maintainability and versatility.

Dubai's chiefs perceived the unpredictability of depending entirely on limited regular assets and decisively put resources into areas like the travel industry, land, money, and innovation. This expansion protected Dubai from monetary shocks as well as situated the city as a diverse worldwide player.

Foundation and Network: The Operations Nexus

Dubai's development as an exchange and development center point is intently attached to its obligation to building elite foundation. The Dubai Global Air terminal, one of the most active on the planet, fills in as a significant passage interfacing East and West. Its essential area works with the development of products and individuals, making Dubai a global travel center point.

The Jebel Ali Port, one of the biggest holder ports worldwide, supplements the city's flight foundation. With cutting edge offices and an extensive free zone contiguous the port, Jebel Ali works with consistent coordinated operations and has turned into a central participant in worldwide exchange. The advancement of the Dubai Strategies Passage, associating Jebel Ali Port to Al Maktoum Worldwide Air terminal, further improves Dubai's calculated abilities.

Furthermore, the city's obligation to development in transportation is obvious in projects like the Dubai Metro, a driverless quick travel framework that facilitates blockage as well as improves network inside the city. These foundation improvements highlight Dubai's commitment to establishing a climate that upholds the progression of merchandise, administrations, and thoughts.

Dubai's Worldwide Exchange Position:

Dubai's essential area, joined with its vigorous foundation, has situated the city as a worldwide exchange and once again trade center point. The Dubai Office of Business and Industry effectively advances exchange and business exercises, working with associations among neighborhood and worldwide endeavors. The city's essential organizations with different nations and locales further add to its job as a scaffold for worldwide exchange.

The Dubai Multi Products Center (DMCC), laid out in 2002, has arisen as a central member in working with the exchange of items like gold, precious stones, and tea. It gives a stage to organizations to lay down a good foundation for themselves in a flourishing biological system, utilizing Dubai's upper hands. The DMCC's drives, including the Dubai Gold and Precious stone Trades, have set the city's situation in the worldwide items market.

The yearly GITEX Innovation Week, held in Dubai, unites innovation aficionados, new businesses, and industry pioneers from around the world. It fills in as a stage for displaying developments and investigating organizations in the consistently advancing innovation area. The outcome of occasions like GITEX mirrors Dubai's obligation to encouraging a climate where mechanical headways are embraced as well as effectively advanced.

Business and Advancement Biological system:

Dubai's job as an exchange and development center point reaches out past worldwide partnerships to embrace business venture and advancement at the grassroots level. The foundation of startup hatcheries and gas pedals, for example, in5 and the Dubai Future Gas pedals program, has made a prolific ground for new businesses and trailblazers to flourish.

The Dubai Future Establishment, sent off in 2016, represents the city's obligation to situating itself at the very front of advancement. The establishment centers around forming the future through drives like the Exhibition hall Representing things to come, a task that joins workmanship, science, and innovation to investigate the conceivable outcomes that lie ahead. These drives are basic to Dubai's way of life as a city that embraces development as well as effectively develops an environment that cultivates it.

The city's facilitating of the World Exhibition in 2020, a worldwide occasion that features developments and thoughts from around the world, further stresses Dubai's obligation to being a center for imagination and ground breaking. The Exhibition is a demonstration of the city's faith in the force of coordinated effort and information trade to shape a superior future.

Brilliant City Drives:

Dubai's yearnings as an exchange and development center are interlaced with its shrewd city drives. The Shrewd Dubai project, sent off in 2013, expects to change the city into a worldwide forerunner in savvy city rehearses. The execution of blockchain innovation in taxpayer driven organizations, the presentation of brilliant government applications, and the combination of man-made consciousness are all important for Dubai's excursion towards turning into a mechanically progressed and creative center point.

The city's obligation to supportability is obvious in drives like the Dubai Clean Energy System 2050, which means to make Dubai a worldwide center point for clean energy and a manageable economy. The Mohammed receptacle Rashid Al Maktoum Sun based Park, perhaps of the biggest sun oriented park on the planet, mirrors Dubai's commitment to broadening its energy sources and embracing economical practices.

3.1 Dubai's strategic location as a global business and trade center.

Dubai's Essential Area: A Nexus of Worldwide Business and Exchange

Dubai, arranged at the junction of the Center East, Asia, Europe, and Africa, has arisen as a worldwide business and exchange focus, impelled by its key geological area. The city's change from an unobtrusive exchanging port to a clamoring city is complicatedly connected to its situation as a nexus for worldwide business. This investigation dives into the meaning of Dubai's essential area, looking at how it has molded the city's set of experiences, filled monetary development, and situated Dubai as a basic center point in the worldwide business scene.

Verifiable Establishments: General store to City

Dubai's set of experiences as a general store goes back hundreds of years, with its essential area along the old shipping lanes interfacing the East and the West. The city's area on the southeastern tip of the Middle Eastern Landmass made it a characteristic port for ships exploring the Bedouin Inlet. Its seaside admittance to the Indian Sea situated Dubai as a critical visit for vendors participated in the rewarding zest exchange and different items.

The Dubai Rivulet, a characteristic channel that slices through the core of the city, assumed an essential part in the verifiable exchange exercises. The river gave a protected harbor to ships, working with sea business and laying out Dubai as a center for seaborne exchange. The clamoring waterfront, decorated with customary dhows stacking and dumping merchandise, turned into a demonstration of Dubai's initial monetary importance.

As the worldwide economy developed, Dubai's essential area kept on assuming a pivotal part in its turn of events. The city's rulers perceived the capability of geographic situating and executed strategies cultivated an open and business-accommodating climate. The foundation of the Dubai River as a streamlined commerce zone in the mid twentieth century laid the preparation for Dubai's development into a worldwide exchanging center.

Worldwide Door: The Crossing point of Mainlands

Dubai's essential area at the convergence of mainlands positions it as a worldwide passage, giving a scaffold between the East and the West. The city's vicinity to Europe, Asia, and Africa makes it an ideal gathering point for organizations trying to lay out a traction in numerous business sectors. This geographic benefit has been an impetus for the city's financial expansion and worldwide unmistakable quality.

The Dubai Worldwide Air terminal, perhaps of the most active air terminal on the planet, epitomizes the city's job as a worldwide passage. With its essential area among Europe and Asia, the air terminal fills in as a urgent center point for worldwide flights. Its best in class offices and productive tasks have made it a favored travel point for voyagers and a strategic center for the development of merchandise.

Dubai's oceanic network is similarly vital to its worldwide situating. The Jebel Ali Port, one of the biggest holder ports around the world, works with the development of merchandise among East and West. The port's essential area along significant transportation courses has added to Dubai's noticeable quality in worldwide exchange. Furthermore, the Dubai Coordinated factors Passage, connecting Jebel Ali Port to Al Maktoum Worldwide Air terminal, upgrades the city's strategic capacities, making a consistent stream for products on the way.

Vital Intersection: The Financial Effect

Dubai's essential area has had a significant monetary effect, molding its development into an enhanced and strong economy. The city's verifiable dependence on sea exchange has extended to envelop a wide range of businesses, including finance, the travel industry, land, and innovation. The essential situating at the intersection of major financial districts has filled Dubai's monetary development and added to its status as a worldwide business and exchange focus.

The foundation of deregulation zones, like Jebel Ali Free Zone (JAFZA), has been a vital driver of financial expansion. These zones, described by business-accommodating guidelines and impetuses, draw in global enterprises, new companies, and business visionaries trying to use Dubai's competitive edges. The enhancement of the economy past oil and gas has been an essential move to guarantee manageability and flexibility even with financial vacillations.

Dubai's essential area has likewise assumed a urgent part in the city's rise as a monetary center point. The Dubai Worldwide Monetary Center (DIFC), laid out in 2004, fills in as a monetary free zone that draws in global banks, monetary establishments, and venture companies. Its nearness to major developing business sectors and its arrangement with worldwide monetary guidelines position DIFC as a pivotal player in worldwide money.

Worldwide Exchange Organizations: Crossing over Landmasses

Dubai's essential area has worked with the foundation of worldwide exchange organizations, making it a vital participant in global business. The city's obligation to open exchange arrangements and its essential unions with nations and districts all over the planet have situated Dubai as an extension between different economies. International alliances and organizations with nations in the Center East, Asia, Africa, and Europe play additionally upgraded Dubai's part in worldwide exchange.

The Dubai Office of Business and Industry effectively advances exchange and business exercises, working with associations among neighborhood and global endeavors. The chamber's drives, including exchange missions, business gatherings, and systems administration occasions, add to the city's situation as a facilitator of worldwide exchange organizations.

Dubai's facilitating of significant worldwide occasions, for example, the Exhibition 2020, represents its obligation to encouraging worldwide exchange linkages. The exhibition fills in as a stage for countries to feature their developments, items, and social legacy, encouraging joint effort and exchange connections on a worldwide scale. Occasions like these highlight Dubai's job as a gathering point for organizations, business visionaries, and pioneers from around the world.

Strategic Center point: Working with Worldwide Development

Dubai's essential area isn't just invaluable for exchange yet additionally for calculated activities that work with worldwide development. The city's interest in elite framework, including air terminals, seaports, and street organizations, has situated it as a calculated center point with unrivaled network.

The Dubai Planned operations Passage, which coordinates Jebel Ali Port with Al Maktoum Worldwide Air terminal, upgrades the city's abilities in taking care of and moving merchandise. This consistent association among air and ocean courses smoothes out calculated processes, making Dubai an effective and vital place for worldwide stock chains.

Dubai's obligation to development in transportation is clear in projects like the Dubai Metro, a cutting edge and broad public transportation framework. The metro reduces gridlock as well as upgrades the simplicity of development inside the city, adding to its proficiency as a calculated center.

Difficulties and Open doors: Exploring What's to come

While Dubai's essential area has been a foundation of its prosperity, it likewise presents difficulties and open doors as the city explores what's to come. The international scene, financial movements, and headways in innovation present the two difficulties and potential open doors for Dubai's job as a worldwide business and exchange focus.

International strains in the Center East and past can affect worldwide shipping lanes and connections. Dubai's capacity to explore these international difficulties and keep up with its situation as an impartial and open business center will be pivotal for its proceeded with progress.

Headways in innovation, including the ascent of online business and advanced stages, present open doors for Dubai to additional upgrade its job in worldwide exchange. The city's obligation to development, as found in projects like the Gallery Representing things to come, positions it to profit by arising advancements that reclassify the scene of worldwide business.

Environmental change and ecological manageability are turning out to be progressively critical variables in worldwide exchange. Dubai's obligation to manageability, exemplified by drives like the Dubai Clean Energy Procedure 2050, mirrors a consciousness of the need to adjust financial exercises to natural contemplations. Exploring the difficulties presented by environmental change and embracing supportable practices will be essential to Dubai's future as a worldwide business and exchange focus.

3.2 The evolution of free zones and their impact on economic growth.

The Development of Free Zones and Their Effect on Monetary Development

Free zones, assigned regions inside a country with extraordinary monetary guidelines and motivating forces, play had a significant impact in forming the worldwide financial scene. Throughout the long term, these zones have advanced from exploratory financial arrangements to vital instruments for advancing exchange, venture, and modern turn of events. This investigation digs into the development of free zones and their significant effect on financial development, utilizing models from around the world to delineate the groundbreaking force of these exceptional monetary substances.

Verifiable Starting points: An Introduction to Financial Trial and error

The idea of free zones has authentic roots that can be followed back to the mid twentieth 100 years. The main free zone was laid out in Shannon, Ireland, in 1959, as a reaction to the monetary difficulties looked by the district. This noticeable the start of a worldwide investigation, testing that giving organizations an assigned region liberated from specific duties and guidelines could prod monetary turn of events.

The model picked up speed in the next many years, with nations all over the planet taking on comparable methodologies to draw in unfamiliar venture and animate financial development. The goals were clear: to make centers of development, support business, and upgrade a country's seriousness in the worldwide market. The foundation of free zones turned into an amazing asset in the possession of policymakers, empowering them to explore different avenues regarding financial strategies inside a controlled climate.

The Development of Free Zones: A Worldwide Peculiarity

As the advantages of free zones became clear, their fame took off across mainlands. Nations in the Center East, Asia, Europe, and the Americas embraced the idea, fitting it to suit their special monetary and formative necessities. Free zones became meaningful of a country's obligation to cultivating a business-accommodating climate and drawing in global venture.

In the Center East, the Unified Middle Easterner Emirates (UAE) stands apart as a trailblazer in utilizing free zones to drive monetary development. The foundation of the Jebel Ali Free Zone (JAFZA) in Dubai in 1985 denoted a groundbreaking second for the district. JAFZA, with its business-accommodating guidelines, charge exclusions, and cutting edge foundation, turned into a magnet for global enterprises looking for an essential traction in the Center East.

Likewise, China's reception of Extraordinary Monetary Zones (SEZs) in the last part of the 1970s assumed a pivotal part in the country's fast financial rising.

The formation of zones, for example, Shenzhen and Shanghai flagged China's obligation to monetary changes and opening up to unfamiliar venture. These zones became research facilities for testing market-situated approaches, prompting remarkable monetary development and modern turn of events.

Key Qualities of Free Zones:

Free zones share normal qualities that recognize them from the remainder of a nation's region. These include:

Charge Motivations: Free zones regularly offer assessment exclusions or diminished charge rates to draw in organizations. This incorporates exclusions from corporate personal expense, esteem added charge (Tank), and customs obligations on imported products.

Customs Advantages: Products entering or leaving a free zone are in many cases subject to improved on customs techniques, lessening regulatory obstacles and working with smoother exchange.

Administrative Adaptability: Free zones give an administrative climate that is more adaptable than the remainder of the country. This incorporates smoothed out regulatory cycles, streamlined permitting methods, and decreased administrative formality.

Framework: Free zones frequently gloat best in class foundation, including present day transportation offices, correspondence organizations, and modern zones custom fitted to explicit areas.

Unfamiliar Possession: Many free zones permit 100 percent unfamiliar proprietorship, giving an appealing suggestion to worldwide organizations hoping to lay out a presence in another market.

Financial Effect: Impetuses for Development

The financial effect of free zones is multi-layered, impacting different parts of a country's development direction. The accompanying key variables highlight the groundbreaking force of free zones in driving monetary turn of events:

Unfamiliar Direct Speculation (FDI): Free zones are strong magnets for FDI. The blend of duty impetuses, administrative adaptability, and a-list foundation makes an alluring suggestion for worldwide organizations. These zones become central focuses for unfamiliar organizations trying to grow their tasks into new business sectors.

Work Age: The foundation of free zones animates work creation. As organizations rush to these zones, they carry with them open doors for business, driving down joblessness rates and adding to by and large monetary prosperity.

Innovation Move and Advancement: Free zones frequently center around unambiguous areas like innovation, exploration, and improvement. This specialization cultivates a culture of development, empowering the exchange of innovation and information among homegrown and global substances inside the zone.

Expansion of the Economy: Nations dependent on unambiguous enterprises, like oil and gas, frequently utilize free zones as a system for monetary broadening. By drawing in organizations from different areas, countries can diminish reliance on a solitary industry and construct a stronger and adjusted economy.

Upgraded Exchange: Free zones work with worldwide exchange by giving smoothed out customs strategies and calculated benefits. Organizations working inside these zones can import, commodity, and once again send out products effortlessly, adding to expanded exchange volumes.

Examples of overcoming adversity: Analyzing Remarkable Free Zones

A few free zones all over the planet act as brilliant illustrations of the monetary effect and achievement reachable through this model. Looking at a couple of striking cases gives experiences into the different techniques utilized by countries to outfit the capability of free zones.

Jebel Ali Free Zone (JAFZA), Dubai, UAE: JAFZA is one of the biggest and best free zones around the world. It plays had a vital impact in changing Dubai into a worldwide business center. With north of 7,500 organizations from in excess of 100 nations, JAFZA traverses assorted areas, including operations, assembling, and administrations. Its prosperity is credited to a blend of tax breaks, vital area, and top notch framework.

Shenzhen Unique Financial Zone (SEZ), China: Shenzhen, when a little fishing town, changed into a worldwide monetary force to be reckoned with through the foundation of the SEZ in 1980. The zone pulled in unfamiliar venture, prompting quick industrialization and metropolitan turn of events. Shenzhen is presently a significant innovation and development center point, home to a portion of China's biggest tech organizations.

Singapore Freeport: Singapore, currently a worldwide monetary and exchange center, laid out the Singapore Freeport to upgrade its status as a worldwide place for craftsmanship and abundance the executives. The Freeport gives secure and environment controlled capacity for significant resources like craftsmanship, valuable metals, and wine. It use Singapore's standing for security, productive strategies, and solid legitimate structures.

Difficulties and Reactions: Adjusting Development and Guideline

While free zones have shown to be compelling devices for financial development, they are not without difficulties and reactions. Finding some kind of harmony between cultivating development and it is vital to guarantee administrative oversight. A portion of the normal difficulties include:

Chance of Monetary Abberations: The outcome of free zones can now and again prompt financial variations between the zones and the remainder of the country. Guaranteeing that the advantages of financial development are circulated impartially across the whole country is a basic thought.

Potential for Tax Avoidance: The duty impetuses presented in free zones might set out open doors for tax avoidance. Finding some kind of harmony between giving alluring motivations and forestalling maltreatment of the framework requires vigorous administrative systems and worldwide participation.

Work Practices: A few free zones have confronted analysis for work works on, including issues connected with specialist privileges and day to day environments. Guaranteeing fair and moral work rehearses inside the zones is fundamental to tending to these worries.

Ecological Effect: The fast industrialization and improvement related with free zones can have natural results. Offsetting monetary development with supportability and ecological stewardship is a test that requires cautious preparation and guideline.

Overreliance on Unambiguous Areas: A few economies might turn out to be excessively dependent on unambiguous areas inside free zones, possibly presenting them to monetary shocks in the event that those areas face slumps. Broadening procedures are fundamental to alleviate such dangers.

Future Patterns: Savvy Free Zones and Maintainability

As the world develops, so do the ideas and models of free zones. Future patterns demonstrate a shift towards brilliant free zones that influence computerized innovations, man-made consciousness, and supportability rehearses. The fuse of brilliant innovations can improve effectiveness, smooth out processes, and add to a more associated and versatile business climate.

Supportability is likewise arising as a critical thought for the fate of free zones. As worldwide familiarity with natural issues develops, there is a push with the expectation of complimentary zones to embrace feasible practices, green innovations, and eco-accommodating foundation. This shift lines up with the more extensive worldwide plan to address environmental change and advance mindful strategic policies.

3.3 Innovations in technology and sustainability that drive the city's progress.

Developments in Innovation and Manageability: Moving the City's Advancement

Dubai, the gem of the Middle Eastern Landmass, has reliably situated itself at the front line of mechanical headways and supportable works on, exhibiting a guarantee to advance and versatility despite worldwide difficulties. This investigation dives into the developments in innovation and maintainability that have become basic to Dubai's story, molding the city's way of life as a guide of innovation, productivity, and ecological cognizance.

Savvy City Drives: Changing Metropolitan Living

Dubai's excursion towards turning into a savvy city is a demonstration of its visionary initiative and obligation to utilizing innovation to improve its inhabitants and guests. The Savvy Dubai drive, sent off in 2013 under the direction of Sheik Mohammed canister Rashid Al Maktoum, the VP and State head of the UAE and Leader of Dubai, looks to change the city into a worldwide forerunner in shrewd city rehearses.

Key parts of Dubai's savvy city drives include:

Shrewd Government: Dubai's administration has embraced computerized change to upgrade administration conveyance and authoritative productivity. Drives, for example, the DubaiNow application combine taxpayer supported organizations, permitting occupants to get to many administrations consistently, from charge installments to permit reestablishments.

Blockchain Innovation: Dubai means to be the world's first blockchain-controlled government by 2020. Blockchain is being coordinated into different areas, including land, money, and medical services, to improve straightforwardness, security, and effectiveness in exchanges.

Computerized reasoning (artificial intelligence): simulated intelligence is assuming a crucial part in Dubai's shrewd city vision. From carrying out simulated intelligence fueled chatbots for client support to using simulated intelligence in medical services for prescient examination, Dubai is embracing the capability of simulated intelligence to work on the personal satisfaction for its occupants.

Web of Things (IoT): Dubai's obligation to IoT is clear in projects like the Brilliant Dubai Stage, which associates different city administrations and information sources. IoT is sent for savvy transportation, squander the executives, and energy protection, adding to a more associated and productive metropolitan climate.

Shrewd Portability: Dubai is putting vigorously in savvy transportation answers for mitigate blockage and upgrade versatility. The Dubai Metro, a driverless and completely computerized quick travel framework, is a brilliant illustration of the city's obligation to reasonable and productive public transportation.

These brilliant city drives on the whole add to Dubai's standing as a worldwide center point for development and innovation, where state of the art arrangements are coordinated into the texture of day to day existence.

Economical Works on: Sustaining a Greener Tomorrow

Dubai's obligation to maintainability is apparent in its endeavors to offset quick metropolitan advancement with natural obligation. The city's chiefs perceive the significance of taking on maintainable practices to safeguard regular assets and make a versatile and eco-accommodating metropolitan scene.

Dubai Clean Energy Procedure 2050: A milestone drive, the Dubai Clean Energy System 2050 expects to make Dubai a worldwide center for clean energy and a reasonable economy. The methodology focuses on a broadening of the energy blend, fully intent on creating 75% of Dubai's complete power from clean energy sources by 2050. The Mohammed canister Rashid Al Maktoum Sun oriented Park, perhaps of the biggest sun based park on the planet, is a lead project under this technique.

Energy-Effective Structures: Dubai has carried out tough guidelines for energy-proficient structures, with the goal of decreasing fossil fuel byproducts and advancing reasonable development rehearses. The Al Maktoum Worldwide Air terminal, Dubai Edge, and Burj Khalifa are instances of designs planned with an emphasis on energy effectiveness.

Water Protection: As a desert city confronting water shortage challenges, Dubai has carried out imaginative answers for water preservation. The utilization of treated sewage emanating for arranging and water system, close by the execution of savvy water system frameworks, mirrors the city's obligation to feasible water the board.

Green Structure Guidelines: Dubai's Green Structure Guidelines and Determinations intend to advance supportable structure rehearses. The city supports the development of green structures that consolidate energy-proficient plans, sustainable power sources, and harmless to the ecosystem materials.

Biodiversity Preservation: Regardless of being a quickly developing metropolitan community, Dubai puts significance on protecting its normal biological systems. The Dubai Desert Protection Save, laid out in 2003, is an illustration of the city's obligation to biodiversity preservation. The save fills in as a safeguarded region for local vegetation, permitting occupants and guests to encounter the normal excellence of the desert.

Sustainable power Drives: Bridling the Force of the Sun

Dubai's quest for sustainable power is exemplified by aggressive drives that bridle the plentiful sunlight based assets of the locale. The Mohammed container Rashid Al Maktoum Sun oriented Park, sent off in 2012, is a historic venture that underlines Dubai's obligation to turning into a worldwide forerunner in environmentally friendly power. The sun based park is intended to deliver 5,000 megawatts (MW) of clean energy by 2030, fundamentally adding to the city's perfect energy objectives.

The sun oriented park incorporates a few key parts:

Photovoltaic Sun powered chargers: The sun based park integrates photovoltaic sunlight based chargers that convert daylight into power. The sweeping cluster of sun powered chargers tackles the sun's energy proficiently, creating perfect and supportable power.

Concentrated Sun based Power (CSP): The sun based park incorporates Concentrated Sun powered Power innovation, which utilizations mirrors or focal points to think daylight onto a little region, delivering high-temperature heat. This intensity is then used to produce power, offering a reciprocal way to deal with conventional photovoltaic innovation.

Energy Capacity: The sun oriented park incorporates energy capacity answers for address the irregularity of sun based power. Batteries and high level stockpiling innovations guarantee a predictable and solid inventory of clean energy, in any event, during times of low daylight.

Advancement Center: The Sun powered Advancement Community: The Sun based Development Place inside the sun oriented park fills in as an innovative work center, cultivating advancement in sun based innovations. It advances coordinated effort among nearby and global specialists, adding to progressions in the field of environmentally friendly power.

Dubai's obligation to environmentally friendly power stretches out past the sun oriented park, with plans to investigate other clean energy sources like breeze and hydroelectric power. These drives add to the city's maintainability objectives as well as position Dubai as a worldwide forerunner in the progress to a low-carbon future.

Coordination of Manageability in Metropolitan Plan: The Practical City

The Economical City, situated on the edges of Dubai, is a spearheading illustration of practical metropolitan turn of events. Imagined as a model for earth cognizant living, the city incorporates state of the art innovations and reasonable practices to make an amicable and eco-accommodating local area.

Key elements of The Manageable City include:

Sunlight based Power Combination: The Feasible City consolidates sun powered chargers across its framework, creating sustainable power to control homes and offices. The coordination of sunlight based power mirrors the city's obligation to clean energy and diminishing reliance on traditional sources.

Green Spaces and Farming: The city focuses on green spaces and horticulture, advancing an association with nature and feasible food creation. Local area ranches, housetop gardens, and green halls add to a better and more supportable metropolitan climate.

Electric Vehicle Charging Foundation: The Feasible City empowers manageable transportation by giving broad electric vehicle charging framework. This drive lines up with Dubai's more extensive objectives of lessening fossil fuel byproducts and advancing eco-accommodating versatility arrangements.

Squander The executives: A complete waste administration framework guarantees the effective arranging, reusing, and removal of waste inside The Supportable City. This obligation to mindful waste administration mirrors Dubai's more extensive endeavors to limit its ecological impression.

Shrewd Home Innovations: Inhabitants of The Practical City benefit from savvy home innovations that upgrade energy utilization, improve productivity, and add to a maintainable way of life. These advances represent the combination of development and supportability in metropolitan living.

The Maintainable City fills in as a living research facility, showing the possibility of economical practices in a cutting edge metropolitan setting. It addresses an outline for future metropolitan turns of events, both in Dubai and universally, stressing the significance of natural obligation despite urbanization.

Chapter 4

"The Desert Blooms: Green Initiatives"

The Desert Blossoms: Green Drives Changing Dubai's Scene

In the core of the Middle Eastern Promontory, where the huge span of desert meets the sky-penetrating horizon, Dubai has arisen as a worldwide city that opposes geological chances as well as trailblazers supportable practices to change its dry scene. This investigation digs into the green drives that have flourished in Dubai, cultivating an amicable connection between metropolitan turn of events and natural protection.

A Green Vision In the midst of the Hills: The Dubai Clean Energy Methodology 2050

At the front of Dubai's obligation to supportability is the Dubai Clean Energy Methodology 2050, a visionary drive that plans to situate the city as a worldwide forerunner in clean energy and manageability. Sent off by His Greatness Sheik Mohammed canister Rashid Al Maktoum, the VP and State leader of the UAE and Leader of Dubai, the system sets aggressive focuses to expand the energy blend and diminish the city's carbon impression.

The critical mainstays of the Dubai Clean Energy Procedure 2050 include:

Energy Proficiency: The procedure focuses on a 30% improvement in energy effectiveness by 2030, underscoring the significance of upgrading energy utilization across different areas. This obligation to effectiveness lines up with Dubai's objective of making a maintainable and asset productive metropolitan climate.

Sustainable power: Dubai intends to create 75% of its complete power from clean energy sources by 2050. The Mohammed canister Rashid Al Maktoum Sunlight based Park, one of the biggest sun oriented stops universally, assumes a significant part in accomplishing this objective. The sun based park bridles the bountiful daylight of the desert to produce perfect and sustainable power.

Carbon Impartiality: Dubai tries to turn into a carbon-unbiased city by 2050, balancing its fossil fuel byproducts through a mix of maintainable practices and carbon catch drives. This responsibility mirrors an all encompassing way to deal with ecological stewardship.

The Dubai Clean Energy Technique 2050 not just highlights the city's commitment to moderating environmental change yet in addition positions Dubai as a good example for other metropolitan habitats trying to offset fast improvement with natural obligation.

Sun based Power: Enlightening the City with Supportable Energy

Vital to Dubai's green drives is the tackling of sun based power, an asset plentiful in the desert scene. The Mohammed canister Rashid Al Maktoum Sun oriented Park remains as a demonstration of the city's obligation to sun powered energy for a great scope. With an aggressive objective of delivering 5,000 megawatts (MW) of clean energy by 2030, the sun based park is a leader project adding to the broadening of Dubai's energy sources.

Key highlights of the Mohammed container Rashid Al Maktoum Sunlight based Park include:

Photovoltaic Sun powered chargers: The sun oriented park integrates immense ranges of photovoltaic sunlight based chargers, changing over daylight into power. These boards, decisively situated across the extensive park, amplify sun powered energy catch and contribute altogether to Dubai's perfect energy creation.

Concentrated Sunlight based Power (CSP): Supplementing photovoltaic innovation, the sun oriented park incorporates Concentrated Sun oriented Power (CSP) frameworks. CSP uses mirrors or focal points to concentrate daylight onto a little region, creating high-temperature heat. This intensity is then used to deliver steam and drive turbines for power age.

Imaginative Capacity Arrangements: Perceiving the discontinuous idea of sun based power, the sun oriented park incorporates progressed energy capacity arrangements. Batteries and capacity innovations store overabundance energy created during top daylight hours, guaranteeing a steady and dependable power supply in any event, during times of low daylight.

Innovative work Center: The sun oriented park incorporates a Sun based Development Community, filling in as a center for innovative work in sun powered advances. This middle cultivates joint effort among nearby and worldwide specialists, driving headways in the field of environmentally friendly power.

Dubai's obligation to sunlight based power reaches out past huge scope projects, with sun powered chargers coordinated into different metropolitan designs and drives. The city embraces sun based innovation as a wellspring of clean energy as well as an image of its commitment to practical metropolitan turn of events.

Green Structures: Molding a Manageable Horizon

Dubai's famous horizon, decorated with transcending high rises and engineering wonders, is progressively characterized by a promise to green structure norms. The city perceives that the development and activity of structures contribute fundamentally to energy utilization and natural effect. As a reaction, Dubai has executed severe guidelines to advance feasible structure rehearses.

Key components of Dubai's green structure drives include:

Energy-Effective Plans: Green structures in Dubai consolidate energy-productive plans that limit energy utilization. This incorporates elements like ideal direction, superior execution glass veneers, and concealing frameworks to decrease the dependence on fake cooling.

Environmentally friendly power Reconciliation: A portion of Dubai's noticeable designs grandstand the mix of environmentally friendly power sources. Sunlight based chargers, wind turbines, and other practical advances are integrated into building plans to produce clean energy on location.

Green Structure Guidelines: Dubai has laid out exhaustive Green Structure Guidelines and Particulars, illustrating the principles for supportable development. These guidelines cover different angles, including energy productivity, water preservation, indoor ecological quality, and the utilization of harmless to the ecosystem materials.

Supportable Confirmation: Dubai urges designers to acquire manageability affirmations for their ventures. The Administration in Energy and Natural Plan (LEED) certificate and the Dubai Supportable Structure Mark are instances of projects that perceive and advance maintainable structure rehearses.

The Burj Khalifa, the world's tallest structure, epitomizes Dubai's obligation to green structure guidelines. The pinnacle integrates energy-effective advances, water-saving measures, and waste reusing frameworks. Likewise, the Dubai Edge, a cutting edge compositional milestone, incorporates feasible highlights, adding to the city's endeavors to shape a horizon that reflects ecological cognizance.

Metropolitan Plant life: Desert spring In the midst of the Substantial Wilderness

Dubai's undertaking to offset metropolitan advancement with vegetation is clear in its obligation to making metropolitan desert gardens. The city perceives the significance of green spaces in improving the personal satisfaction for occupants and guests while adding to natural supportability.

Key drives advancing metropolitan plant life include:

Stops and Gardens: Dubai brags an organization very much kept up with parks and gardens, giving occupants spaces for entertainment and unwinding. Stops like Safa Park and Zabeel Park offer green spans as well as consolidate economical finishing rehearses.

Green Hallways: Dubai has carried out green passages, improving the stylish allure of metropolitan regions while advancing biodiversity. These hallways, frequently fixed with trees and plants, add to the city's endeavors to make a more maintainable and lovely metropolitan climate.

Vertical Nurseries: In a city where land is a valuable product, vertical nurseries have turned into a well known answer for bring vegetation into metropolitan spaces. High rises and business structures feature creative vertical nurseries, adding to the city's green drives.

Local area Homesteads: Dubai energizes local area cultivating drives, permitting occupants to partake in economical agribusiness effectively. These people group ranches add to nearby food creation as well as encourage a feeling of local area and ecological mindfulness.

Dubai's obligation to metropolitan vegetation stretches out past style, enveloping the multi-layered advantages of green spaces, including further developed air quality, upgraded biodiversity, and a stronger and reasonable metropolitan biological system.

Squander The executives: Towards a Roundabout Economy

Dubai perceives the significance of capable waste administration in its excursion towards manageability. The city has carried out drives to decrease squander age, advance reusing, and move towards a round economy.

Key parts of Dubai's waste administration drives include:

Squander Decrease Measures: Dubai empowers squander decrease at the source by advancing maintainable practices. This incorporates missions to diminish single-use plastics, advance treating the soil, and bring issues to light about the ecological effect of unreasonable utilization.

Reusing Projects: Dubai has laid out complete reusing projects to redirect recyclable materials from landfills. The city advances the reusing of paper, glass, plastics, and electronic waste, adding to the preservation of regular assets.

Squander to-Energy Activities: Dubai investigates squander to-energy projects as a feature of its maintainable waste administration technique. These undertakings expect to change over non-recyclable waste into energy, lining up with the city's spotless energy objectives.

Round Economy Drives: Dubai is progressively embracing the idea of a round economy, where assets are reused, reused, and reused. Drives to advance circularity incorporate the improvement of reasonable bundling and the consolation of capable utilization rehearses.

By tending to squander the board exhaustively, Dubai intends to limit its ecological impression and add to the worldwide change towards a more reasonable and round way to deal with asset the executives.

4.1 Dubai's commitment to sustainability and environmental conservation.

Dubai's Obligation to Supportability and Ecological Protection: A Visionary Desert spring in the Desert

In the core of the Middle Eastern Promontory, where the sun-doused desert meets the sparkling waters of the Persian Bay, Dubai has arisen as a worldwide monetary center point as well as a pioneer in reasonable turn of events and ecological preservation. This investigation dives into Dubai's immovable obligation to supportability, following the city's excursion from a desert scene to a visionary desert garden that places ecological cognizance at the front of its development.

A Visionary Initiative: Outlining the Course for Maintainability

Dubai's obligation to maintainability is unpredictably woven into the texture of its administration, driven by the visionary initiative of His Excellency Sheik Mohammed canister Rashid Al Maktoum, the VP and Head of the state of the UAE and Leader of Dubai. Sheik Mohammed's ground breaking approach perceives the double liability of guaranteeing financial thriving while at the same time defending the climate for people in the future.

The foundation of Dubai's maintainability vision is the Dubai Clean Energy System 2050, a thorough guide that frames aggressive objectives across key mainstays of energy proficiency, sustainable power, and carbon nonpartisanship. Imagined as a groundbreaking drive, the procedure positions Dubai as a worldwide innovator in clean energy, setting a model for different urban areas wrestling with the difficulties of urbanization and natural effect.

Environmentally friendly power Upset: The Mohammed container Rashid Al Maktoum Sun based Park

At the core of Dubai's obligation to environmentally friendly power lies the Mohammed receptacle Rashid Al Maktoum Sunlight based Park, a fantastic undertaking that has become inseparable from the city's drive towards maintainability. Spreading over huge spans of desert, the sun based park is a demonstration of Dubai's hug of its most bountiful regular asset - daylight.

The sunlight based park utilizes a multi-layered way to deal with tackle sun oriented energy, consolidating both photovoltaic sunlight based chargers and Concentrated Sunlight based Power (CSP) innovation. The sheer size of the task is faltering, with plans to produce 5,000 megawatts (MW) of clean energy by 2030. This incorporates not just giving ability to meet the city's developing energy needs yet in addition contributing abundance energy to the lattice.

Past sheer energy creation, the sun powered park fills in as an innovative work center point through the Sun oriented Development Community. Here, nearby and world-wide specialists team up on progressing sunlight based advances, driving development in the mission for more productive and economical energy arrangements.

Energy Proficiency: A Mainstay of Dubai's Manageability Model

Dubai's obligation to supportability reaches out past the creation of clean energy to the productive usage of assets. The Dubai Clean Energy Procedure 2050 puts serious areas of strength for an on further developing energy proficiency, with an objective of accomplishing a 30% improvement by 2030.

Brilliant city drives assume a urgent part in accomplishing energy proficiency objectives. From wise structure plans that improve regular lighting and cooling to the execution of shrewd networks and meters, Dubai use state of the art advancements to upgrade the city's general energy execution. The reconciliation of man-made brainpower (simulated intelligence) and the Web of Things (IoT) in metropolitan foundation further adds to constant checking and versatile energy the executives.

Dubai's obligation to energy proficiency is reflected in the retrofitting of existing structures to fulfill green guidelines and the execution of severe guidelines for new developments. The city's horizon, decorated with transcending structures, becomes an image of monetary ability as well as a demonstration of economical design and mindful asset use.

Green Structure Norms: Forming the Horizon Capably

Dubai's famous horizon, described by compositional wonders like the Burj Khalifa and the Burj Al Middle Easterner, isn't just a demonstration of the city's financial ability yet in addition to its obligation to green structure guidelines. The authority perceives that the development and activity of structures contribute essentially to energy utilization, emanations, and generally speaking natural effect.

The Green Structure Guidelines and Particulars set by Dubai give a system to feasible development rehearses. From energy-productive plans that limit the dependence on counterfeit cooling to the consolidation of sustainable power sources, green structures in Dubai stick to a comprehensive methodology towards ecological obligation.

Noticeable designs, including the Burj Khalifa, represent the combination of manageable highlights. Energy-productive glass exteriors, ideal direction to use normal daylight, and water-saving measures add to diminishing the natural impression of these design monsters.

Dubai's commitment to green structure norms stretches out past individual designs to whole networks. Maintainable metropolitan arranging standards are applied to make eco-accommodating areas that focus on energy proficiency, green spaces, and a top notch of life for inhabitants.

Water Protection: Supporting Manageability in a Bone-dry Climate

In a city encompassed by desert, water protection turns into a basic part of Dubai's manageability system. Confronting difficulties of water shortage and dry environment, the authority has executed imaginative answers for guarantee mindful water utilization and protection.

Dubai's way to deal with water preservation incorporates:

Treated Sewage Emanating (TSE): Dubai use treated sewage profluent for non-consumable purposes, like water system and arranging. This drive decreases the interest on freshwater assets, adding to supportability in a locale where water is a valuable ware.

Brilliant Water system Frameworks: The execution of shrewd water system frameworks is a vital part of Dubai's water protection endeavors. These frameworks use sensors and information examination to advance watering plans in light of weather patterns, soil dampness levels, and plant necessities, in this way limiting water wastage.

Desalination Development: While desalination has customarily been a critical wellspring of freshwater in the district, Dubai investigates advancements in desalination advancements to improve proficiency and lessen natural effect. Innovative work drives center around reasonable desalination rehearses that line up with the city's obligation to natural stewardship.

Water Protection Mindfulness: Dubai effectively connects with its occupants and organizations in water preservation mindfulness crusades. Instructive drives stress capable water use works on, empowering an aggregate exertion towards manageability.

By embracing a diverse way to deal with water preservation, Dubai endeavors to adjust the requests of metropolitan improvement with the need to save scant water assets, making an economical model for water the board in bone-dry conditions.

Biodiversity Protection: Supporting Nature in the Metropolitan Wilderness

Notwithstanding its fast urbanization, Dubai puts areas of strength for an on saving its normal biological systems and biodiversity. The Dubai Desert Protection Hold, laid out in 2003, remains as a demonstration of the city's obligation to keeping a sensitive harmony among improvement and ecological preservation.

The hold fills in as a safeguarded region for local vegetation, giving a natural surroundings to animal categories that have adjusted to the unforgiving desert climate. Directed visits and eco-accommodating exercises inside the save permit occupants and guests to encounter the regular excellence of the desert while bringing issues to light about the significance of biodiversity protection.

Moreover, Dubai's green drives incorporate the formation of green halls and metropolitan green spaces, adding to the generally speaking biological strength of the city. These drives not just improve the tasteful allure of metropolitan regions yet in addition give pockets of biodiversity amidst the substantial wilderness.

Squander The executives: Towards a Roundabout Economy

Dubai perceives the significance of dependable waste administration in its excursion towards manageability. The city has executed drives to limit squander age, advance reusing, and move towards a round economy.

Key parts of Dubai's waste administration drives include:

Squander Decrease Measures: Dubai supports squander decrease at the source through open mindfulness crusades. Drives center around lessening single-use plastics, advancing dependable utilization, and empowering the reception of eco-accommodating practices.

Reusing Projects: Dubai has laid out extensive reusing programs that cover a scope of materials, including paper, glass, plastics, and electronic waste. The accentuation on reusing intends to redirect materials from landfills and preserve significant assets.

Round Economy Drives: Dubai is at the very front of investigating round economy standards. This includes planning items with an emphasis on reuse, reusing, and reusing. The shift towards a round economy lines up with Dubai's more extensive manageability objectives.

By tending to squander the board extensively, Dubai plans to limit its ecological impression and add to the worldwide change towards a more feasible and round way to deal with asset the executives.

4.2 Landscaping and greening projects that challenge the desert stereotype.

Arranging and Greening Ventures: Changing the Desert Generalization in Dubai

In the core of the Bedouin Promontory, where the brilliant sands of the desert stretch as may be obvious, Dubai has embraced a striking excursion to challenge the conventional generalization of parched scenes. Through visionary arranging and greening projects, the city has changed its environmental factors, resisting the desert's unforgiving circumstances and making lavish, maintainable conditions. This investigation dives into the aggressive drives that have reclassified Dubai's scene and made ready for a greener, more dynamic future.

Greening the Desert: The Aggressive Dubai Desert Preservation Save

At the very front of Dubai's endeavors to challenge the desert generalization is the Dubai Desert Preservation Save (DDCR). Laid out in 2003, this far reaching save traverses more than 225 square kilometers, addressing a pledge to protecting the district's novel biodiversity and advancing feasible desert environments.

Key highlights of the Dubai Desert Protection Hold include:

Protection of Local Greenery: The DDCR fills in as a safe-haven for a different cluster of local plant and creature species that have adjusted to the brutal desert climate. Imperiled species, for example, the Bedouin oryx and sand gazelle track down asylum inside the save, featuring Dubai's devotion to biodiversity preservation.

Eco-Accommodating The travel industry: The save permits guests to encounter the desert's regular magnificence while limiting natural effect. Directed visits, led with an emphasis on eco-accommodating practices, give a brief look into the interesting vegetation of the desert, encouraging natural mindfulness and training.

Examination and Protection: The DDCR fills in as a middle for exploration and preservation drives. Joint efforts with neighborhood and worldwide specialists add to a more profound comprehension of desert biological systems and backing endeavors to safeguard and support the locale's regular legacy.

By laying out the Dubai Desert Protection Hold, Dubai has saved its common habitat as well as tested assumptions about deserts as ungracious scenes. The save remains as a demonstration of the city's obligation to manageable turn of events and dependable the travel industry.

Metropolitan Desert spring: Safa Park and Green Spaces

Dubai's obligation to testing the desert generalization reaches out past protection stores to the core of the actual city. Safa Park, situated amidst the clamoring metropolitan scene, epitomizes Dubai's vision of making green spaces that give relief from the substantial wilderness.

Key parts of Safa Park and other green spaces in Dubai include:

Rich Arranging: Safa Park highlights lavish plant life, including manicured yards, lively blossom beds, and tree-lined pathways. This intentional finishing not just improves the visual allure of the recreation area yet in addition makes a quiet desert spring for occupants and guests.

Sporting Conveniences: Green spaces in Dubai are intended to offer a scope of sporting conveniences. Safa Park, for instance, incorporates running tracks, jungle gyms, and excursion regions, giving open doors to outside exercises and local area commitment.

Reasonable Practices: Dubai consolidates manageable practices in the support of its green spaces. Water-proficient water system frameworks, the utilization of local and dry spell safe plant species, and eco-accommodating finishing strategies add to asset preservation in a district where water is a valuable item.

These metropolitan desert springs challenge the thought of a desolate desert city, displaying Dubai's obligation to making an amicable harmony between metropolitan turn of events and vegetation. The city's way to deal with finishing advances ecological manageability as well as upgrades the general prosperity of its occupants.

The Marvel Nursery: Sprouts in the Desert

Without a doubt one of the most notable finishing projects in Dubai is the Dubai Supernatural occurrence Nursery, an organic scene that resists the desert's standing for aridity. Sent off in 2013, the Marvel Nursery is a spectacular showcase of lively blossoms, complex plans, and themed gardens, making it the world's biggest regular bloom garden.

Key highlights of the Dubai Wonder Nursery include:

Occasional Blossoms: The Supernatural occurrence Nursery is an occasional fascination, regularly open from November to April when the weather conditions is helpful for flower shows. During this period, a large number of blossoms in a bunch of varieties and assortments sprout, making an entrancing embroidery in the core of the desert.

Creative Plans: The nursery highlights imaginative plans and figures made altogether of blossoms. From heart-molded entrances to life-sized copies of notable milestones, the Marvel Nursery exhibits the imaginative capability of arranging in changing parched spaces into energetic, living show-stoppers.

Manageability Drives: Regardless of the extreme showcase, the Marvel Nursery consolidates maintainable practices in its tasks. Water-proficient water system frameworks, reused water, and endeavors to limit natural effect mirror Dubai's obligation to mindful finishing even in apparently excessive activities.

The Wonder Nursery fills in as a demonstration of Dubai's capacity to transform difficulties into valuable open doors. By making a lavish, flower heaven in the core of the desert, the city challenges assumptions about the restrictions of finishing in dry conditions.

Greening the Upward: Vertical Nurseries and Reasonable Engineering

Dubai's obligation to testing the desert generalization expands upward, with imaginative tasks that integrate vegetation into the actual texture of its engineering scene. Vertical nurseries, otherwise called living walls, have turned into a conspicuous element of reasonable design in the city.

Key parts of vertical nurseries in Dubai include:

High rise Vegetation: A few high rises in Dubai have embraced the idea of vertical nurseries on their exteriors. These living walls increase the value of the structures as well as add to natural manageability by giving shade, diminishing intensity ingestion, and further developing air quality.

Reasonable Structure Practices: Vertical nurseries line up with Dubai's green structure norms, which accentuate supportability in development. Structures consolidating vertical gardens frequently coordinate energy-productive plans, utilize harmless to the ecosystem materials, and influence sustainable power sources.

Air Sanitization: Vertical nurseries assume a part in cleaning the air by engrossing poisons and delivering oxygen. This adds to establishing better metropolitan conditions, especially in thickly populated regions where air quality can be a worry.

Projects like the Oasia Inn Downtown, with its verdant façade of flowing plant life, epitomize Dubai's obligation to rethinking the visual scene of its metropolitan engineering. Vertical nurseries challenge the customary view of high rises as images of cement and glass, changing them into no nonsense substances that coincide amicably with nature.

Reasonable Desert Scenes: The Al Marmoom Drive

The Al Marmoom Drive is a spearheading project that tries to make feasible desert scenes while protecting the locale's regular legacy. Sent off by the Dubai District, this drive incorporates a large number of ventures pointed toward upgrading biodiversity, advancing eco-accommodating the travel industry, and testing the view of deserts as fruitless scenes.

Key parts of the Al Marmoom Drive include:

Al Marmoom Nature Hold: The drive incorporates the improvement of the Al Marmoom Nature Save, an immense region of desert that has been changed into a safe house for untamed life. The hold is home to an assortment of native widely varied vegetation, giving a one of a kind open door to nature devotees to investigate the desert environment.

Sun oriented Power Desert spring: In accordance with Dubai's obligation to environmentally friendly power, the Al Marmoom Drive includes the improvement of a Sun based Power Desert garden. This task incorporates sun powered chargers with the desert scene, bridling the plentiful daylight to create clean energy while limiting the effect on the environment.

Maintainable The travel industry: The drive advances reasonable the travel industry works on, empowering guests to see the value in the excellence of the desert while regarding its fragile equilibrium. Eco-accommodating exercises, directed visits, and instructive projects expect to bring issues to light about the significance of desert protection.

By consolidating biological conservation with practical turn of events, the Al Marmoom Drive difficulties the generalization of deserts as dormant fields and shows Dubai's obligation to making versatile, flourishing scenes as one with nature.

4.3 Renewable energy initiatives and their impact on the city's future.

Environmentally friendly power Drives: Controlling Dubai's Practical Future

In the steadily developing scene of Dubai, where the desert sun projects its resolute beams, the city has left on a groundbreaking excursion toward a reasonable future through aggressive sustainable power drives. This investigation dives into the momentous tasks that bridle the force of the sun, the breeze, and inventive innovations to meet the city's developing energy requests as well as make ready for a cleaner, greener, and stronger Dubai.

The Sun as a Force to be reckoned with: The Mohammed canister Rashid Al Maktoum Sun powered Park

At the front of Dubai's environmentally friendly power upheaval stands the notable Mohammed container Rashid Al Maktoum Sunlight based Park. Laid out as perhaps of the biggest sun powered park on the planet, this visionary undertaking is a demonstration of Dubai's obligation to enhancing its energy blend and diminishing its carbon impression.

Key parts of the Mohammed container Rashid Al Maktoum Sun based Park include:

Photovoltaic Sun powered chargers: The sun oriented park is furnished with huge swaths of photovoltaic sunlight based chargers that outfit the plentiful daylight of the desert to produce perfect and feasible power. The productivity of these boards has worked on throughout the long term, adding to the recreation area's ability to create megawatts of sun based power.

Concentrated Sunlight based Power (CSP) Innovation: Supplementing customary photovoltaic innovation, the sun oriented park integrates Concentrated Sun based Power (CSP) frameworks. These frameworks use mirrors or focal points to focus daylight onto a little region, creating high-temperature heat. This intensity is then used to deliver steam and drive turbines for power age.

Creative Capacity Arrangements: Perceiving the irregular idea of sunlight based power, the sun oriented park incorporates progressed energy capacity arrangements. These capacity frameworks, for example, huge scope batteries, store overabundance energy produced during top daylight hours, guaranteeing a steady and dependable power supply in any event, during times of low daylight.

Development Plans: The sun oriented park is ceaselessly growing to expand its ability and further outfit the sun's energy. With aggressive focuses to produce a critical piece of Dubai's power from inexhaustible sources, the Mohammed canister Rashid

Al Maktoum Sun based Park assumes an essential part in the city's change to a more feasible energy future.

By taking advantage of the tremendous capability of sunlight based energy, Dubai tends to its energy needs as well as contributes altogether to worldwide endeavors to battle environmental change and lessen dependence on petroleum products.

Wind Energy: The Dubai Clean Energy Technique 2050

Notwithstanding sun oriented power, Dubai is effectively investigating the capability of wind energy as a feature of its far reaching Clean Energy Technique 2050. This system sets aggressive focuses to expand the portion of clean energy in the city's complete power yield, showing an all encompassing way to deal with manageability.

Key parts of wind energy drives in Dubai include:

Wind Ranches: Dubai has started plans to lay out coastal and seaward wind homesteads to tackle the energy of the breeze. These ranches, decisively situated to expand wind openness, will add to broadening the city's environmentally friendly power portfolio.

Energy Effectiveness: The Perfect Energy Procedure 2050 underlines the significance of energy proficiency in all areas. By enhancing energy utilization and executing creative advancements, Dubai expects to accomplish a 30% improvement in energy effectiveness by 2030, adding to generally maintainability objectives.

Carbon Impartiality: One of the mainstays of the methodology is accomplishing carbon nonpartisanship by 2050. This includes counterbalancing fossil fuel byproducts through a blend of feasible practices, carbon catch drives, and the expanded utilization of sustainable power sources.

Dubai's obligation to wind energy lines up with its vision for a decent and broadened energy blend, guaranteeing a strong and feasible power supply for the city's future.

Hydrogen Economy: The Green Hydrogen Plant

In a spearheading move towards a hydrogen-controlled future, Dubai has divulged plans for a Green Hydrogen Plant. This aggressive task means to deliver green hydrogen utilizing environmentally friendly power sources, denoting a huge move toward the city's change to a hydrogen-based economy.

Key elements of the Green Hydrogen Plant include:

Electrolysis Innovation: The plant uses progressed electrolysis innovation to part water into hydrogen and oxygen utilizing power created from sustainable sources. This interaction, known as electrolysis, produces green hydrogen without fossil fuel byproducts, situating it as a spotless and manageable energy transporter.

Combination with Sunlight based Power: The Green Hydrogen Plant is incorporated with the Mohammed canister Rashid Al Maktoum Sun oriented Park, guaranteeing an inexhaustible wellspring of power for the electrolysis interaction. This collaboration between sun oriented power and hydrogen creation epitomizes Dubai's all encompassing way to deal with economical energy arrangements.

Applications in Different Areas: Green hydrogen produced by the plant has assorted applications, including transportation, industry, and power age. By cultivating the improvement of a hydrogen economy, Dubai imagines a future where this flexible and clean energy transporter assumes a focal part in diminishing fossil fuel byproducts across areas.

The Green Hydrogen Plant means Dubai's obligation to investigating creative and state of the art answers for an economical energy future. As hydrogen acquires noticeable quality as a central member in the worldwide energy progress, Dubai positions itself at the very front of this groundbreaking excursion.

Influence on Monetary Enhancement and Energy Security

Dubai's interest in sustainable power drives reaches out past natural contemplations to vital financial enhancement and energy security. The city perceives the monetary potential and long haul advantages of changing to a practical energy model.

Monetary Expansion: By putting resources into environmentally friendly power, Dubai means to differentiate its economy past conventional areas like oil and gas. The improvement of a powerful sustainable power industry sets out new position open doors, encourages development, and positions Dubai as a worldwide forerunner in the change to a low-carbon economy.

Energy Security: Reliance on customary energy sources, especially petroleum products, presents dangers to energy security. By embracing renewables, Dubai diminishes its dependence on imported fills, upgrades energy autonomy, and mitigates weaknesses related with changes in worldwide energy markets.

Advancement Center point: Dubai's obligation to environmentally friendly power positions the city as a development center point for practical innovations. The combination of trend setting innovations in sun powered, wind, and hydrogen creation cultivates innovative work, drawing in ability and interests in the thriving green innovation area.

Difficulties and Future Possibilities

While Dubai's environmentally friendly power drives feature huge advancement, challenges endure in the way toward a completely supportable future. The discontinuous idea of sustainable sources, energy capacity abilities, and the requirement for progressing mechanical headways are contemplations that request nonstop consideration.

Irregularity: Sun based and wind energy are discontinuous sources, reliant upon weather patterns. To address this test, Dubai is putting resources into cutting edge energy capacity arrangements, like enormous scope batteries, to store overabundance energy during top creation hours and guarantee a steady power supply.

Energy Capacity: The versatility and effectiveness of energy stockpiling innovations are basic for beating the discontinuity of sustainable sources. Dubai's emphasis on creating progressed energy capacity arrangements mirrors the city's obligation to tending to this test and guaranteeing a dependable and constant power supply.

Innovative Progressions: Continuous innovative work are fundamental for propelling the proficiency and reasonableness of sustainable power advances. Dubai's commitment to development and coordinated effort with global specialists positions the city at the cutting edge of mechanical progressions in the sustainable power area.

Looking forward, Dubai's sustainable power venture is ready for additional extension and advancement. The city's essential vision, as illustrated in the Perfect Energy Technique 2050, mirrors a pledge to accomplishing reasonable turn of events, financial success, and natural stewardship.

Chapter 5

"Luxury and Leisure"

Extravagance and Relaxation: Dubai's Lavishness Reclassified

In the domain of richness and lavishness, Dubai remains as a worldwide symbol of extravagance and recreation, a city that has carefully made a way of life inseparable from loftiness and guilty pleasure. This investigation dives into the luxurious universe of Dubai, where transcending high rises, extravagant retreats, top of the line shopping, and a-list diversion combine to rethink the actual quintessence of extravagance and relaxation.

The Ascent of Rich High rises: An Upward Jungle gym

Dubai's horizon is a demonstration of its immovable quest for building greatness and brazen self importance. Notorious designs like the Burj Khalifa, the world's tallest structure, and the Burj Al Bedouin, a sail-formed wonder roosted on its own island, represent the city's obligation to pushing the limits of plan and designing.

The Burj Khalifa, penetrating the sky at more than 828 meters, isn't only a construction; it's an encapsulation of extravagance living. The upper floors of this compositional wonder house elite homes, corporate suites, and the widely acclaimed Armani Lodging. Occupants and visitors of the Burj Khalifa are blessed to receive unmatched perspectives on the city, the Bedouin Inlet, and the encompassing desert, making a living encounter that rises above the normal.

The Burj Al Middle Easterner, frequently hailed as the main seven-star inn on the planet, takes extravagance higher than ever. Its extravagant insides, decorated with gold leaf and multifaceted mosaics, ooze a demeanor of loftiness. Visitors appreciate customized steward administration, driver driven Rolls-Royce moves, and admittance to the lodging's confidential ocean side on an island solely devoted to Burj Al Bedouin visitors. These transcending structures overwhelm the horizon as well as act as reference points of Dubai's obligation to giving a phenomenal way of life to the individuals who look for the encapsulation of extravagance.

Extravagance Resorts and Islands: Shoreline Lavishness

Dubai's shoreline is a material whereupon the city has painted an embroidery of extravagance resorts, confidential islands, and ocean front plushness. The Palm Jumeirah, a counterfeit archipelago molded like a palm tree, is a work of art of designing and a jungle gym for the princely. Home to super lavish homes, store lodgings, and the famous Atlantis, The Palm, this man-made wonder has become inseparable from ocean side excess.

The Atlantis, with its striking plan and marine-themed design, offers a universe of extravagance and relaxation. From submerged suites with hypnotizing perspectives on marine life to VIP culinary specialist eateries, a waterpark, and a confidential ocean side, Atlantis exemplifies the pith of a selective island retreat. The Palm Jumeirah is a demonstration of Dubai's capacity to change its shoreline into a safe house for those looking for unrivaled ocean side extravagance.

Compared against the horizon is the Burj Al Bedouin Jumeirah Ocean side Lodging, another building pearl that supplements the Burj Al Middle Easterner. This sail-molded structure is a safe house for those wanting ocean front extravagance. The lodging's plan imitates the sail of a dhow, a customary Middle Eastern cruising vessel, and its insides are an orchestra of luxurious materials and contemporary plan. Visitors of the Burj Al Bedouin Jumeirah Ocean side Lodging luxuriate in the greatness of private sea shores, perfect feasting encounters, and unmatched perspectives on the Middle Eastern Bay.

Very good quality Shopping: Retail Treatment Re-imagined

Dubai has reclassified the idea of retail treatment by making shopping objections that take special care of the most insightful preferences. The city's shopping centers are not simply business spaces; they are luxurious features of extravagance brands, state of the art style, and vivid retail encounters.

The Dubai Shopping center, one of the world's biggest shopping and diversion locations, is a microcosm of extravagance. Lodging top of the line stores like Chanel, Gucci, and Louis Vuitton, the shopping center is a famous hub for design devotees. The rambling Design Road inside the shopping center is a committed region for extravagance brands, offering a consistent mix of style and refinement.

Contiguous the Dubai Shopping center is the Souk Al Bahar, a conventional Bedouin market with a contemporary bend. Here, guests can investigate shop stores offering one of a kind high quality items, gems, and custom tailored design things. The juxtaposition of present day extravagance and customary appeal makes Souk Al Bahar a particular shopping objective.

For those looking for a more private and selective experience, The Road at Etihad Pinnacles is a refined objective inside the Jumeirah at Etihad Pinnacles complex. This store shopping road offers an organized determination of global and nearby extravagance brands, making a feeling of eliteness and refinement.

Culinary Excess: A Gastronomic Odyssey

Dubai's culinary scene is a lively embroidery of flavors, surfaces, and culinary craftsmanship. The city's gastronomic scene is set apart by Michelin-featured cafés, VIP gourmet specialists, and eating encounters that rise above the conventional.

Pierchic, settled toward the finish of its own confidential dock in the Middle Eastern Bay, is an exemplification of Dubai's culinary luxury. This overwater café has practical experience in fish and offers all encompassing perspectives on the Bay and the Dubai shore. Eating at Pierchic isn't simply a dinner; it's an excursion into the domains of extravagance, where everything about, the mood to the food, is fastidiously organized for an insightful customers.

The Burj Al Bedouin, with its variety of elite cafés, lifts eating to a fine art. Al Mahara, a submerged eatery with an entrancing aquarium setting, is a demonstration of the city's obligation to pushing the limits of culinary development. Visitors enjoy a gastronomic journey organized by famous culinary specialists, wrapped in a climate that flawlessly mixes extravagance and wantonness.

Dubai's culinary scene isn't restricted to high end food; it stretches out to energetic road food markets and food celebrations that celebrate worldwide flavors. The Dubai Food Celebration, held every year, unites Michelin-featured cooks, food fans, and culinary developments, exhibiting the city's obligation to offering a different and dynamic gastronomic experience.

A-list Diversion: Excess in Execution

Dubai's obligation to amusement is inseparable from lavishness. The city has a-list exhibitions, shows, and occasions that draw in worldwide crowds looking for unrivaled encounters.

The Dubai Drama, with its dazzling plan enlivened by conventional dhow sails, is a social symbol that has a different scope of exhibitions. From show and artful dance to shows by worldwide craftsmen, the Dubai Drama is a demonstration of the city's commitment to encouraging a dynamic expressions and diversion scene.

Worldwide Town, a yearly multicultural celebration, changes into a kaleidoscope of varieties, music, and exhibitions from around the world. This outside party highlights structures addressing various nations, each offering an extraordinary mix of diversion, shopping, and culinary joys. Worldwide Town is a demonstration of Dubai's obligation to praising variety and giving a worldwide stage to social trade.

In the domain of sports and relaxation, Dubai's obligation to excess is exemplified by occasions, for example, the Dubai World Cup, one of the most extravagant horse races on the planet. Held at the Meydan Racecourse, this occasion draws in equestrian devotees, high-profile characters, and the worldwide first class for a day of high-stakes hustling and unmatched extravagance.

5.1 The rise of Dubai as a luxury destination.

The Ascent of Dubai as an Extravagance Objective: A Story of Lavishness and Tastefulness

Dubai's rising as a worldwide extravagance objective is a convincing story that unfurls against the background of a city that has changed from an unassuming exchanging port to an embodiment of richness and tastefulness. This investigation dives into the variables that have pushed Dubai into the echelons of extravagance travel, from notable milestones to top notch cordiality, making a spellbinding embroidery of luxury that coaxes the insightful explorer.

Visionary Metropolitan Turn of events: Molding the Cityscape

At the core of Dubai's transformation into an extravagance objective untruths visionary metropolitan improvement that has molded the cityscape into a cutting edge wonder. The city's horizon, overwhelmed by notable designs like the Burj Khalifa and the Burj Al Bedouin, represents Dubai's obligation to engineering greatness and stylish glory.

The Burj Khalifa, remaining as the world's tallest structure, isn't simply a design win; it's an image of Dubai's desire to arrive at new levels of extravagance. The upper floors of this transcending structure house selective homes, corporate suites, and the prestigious Armani Lodging. Occupants and visitors are blessed to receive unmatched perspectives on the city, the Bedouin Bay, and the huge region of the encompassing desert, offering a living encounter that rises above traditional ideas of plushness.

The Burj Al Bedouin, frequently alluded to as the main seven-star lodging on the planet, is a guide of extravagance that graces the city's shoreline. Its sail-molded outline and rich insides have become inseparable from the lavishness that Dubai addresses. With customized steward administration, escort driven Rolls-Royce moves, and admittance to a confidential ocean side, the Burj Al Bedouin sets the norm for friendliness that takes special care of the most insightful voyagers.

Lovely Cordiality: Luxury Retreats and Rich Hotels

Dubai's neighborliness area assumes a vital part in laying out the city as an extravagance objective. The Palm Jumeirah, a fake archipelago molded like a palm tree, is home to an assortment of super sumptuous hotels that reclassify coastline richness. The Atlantis, The Palm, remains as a demonstration of Dubai's obligation to making vivid and extreme encounters. From submerged suites with all encompassing perspectives on marine life to superstar culinary specialist eateries, a waterpark, and a confidential ocean side, Atlantis exemplifies the substance of a selective island retreat.

Past the palm-bordered archipelago, the Jumeirah Ocean side Inn supplements the notable Burj Al Middle Easterner. With its sail-formed plan reflecting the Bedouin dhow, the inn offers ocean front extravagance on the shores of the Middle Eastern Inlet. Visitors enjoy customized administrations, dazzling eating encounters, and stunning perspectives, making a retreat that consistently mixes style with contemporary solace.

The desert withdraws in Dubai, for example, the Al Maha Desert Resort and Spa and the Bab Al Hoaxes Desert Resort and Spa, present a desert garden of extravagance in the midst of the peaceful territory of the desert. These retreats offer disconnected manors, confidential dive pools, and vivid desert encounters, permitting visitors to loosen up in a climate that radiates complexity and peacefulness.

Top of the line Shopping Event: Retail Mecca for Authorities

Dubai's retail scene is a super charged mix of extravagance brands, creator shops, and state of the art style. The Dubai Shopping center, one of the world's biggest shopping and diversion objections, is a microcosm of plushness. It houses a plenty of very good quality stores, including Chanel, Gucci, and Louis Vuitton, making it a world renowned hub for design fans looking for the most recent patterns and extravagance manifestations.

Neighboring the Dubai Shopping center is Souk Al Bahar, a contemporary translation of a conventional Middle Eastern market. Here, guests can investigate shop stores offering novel high quality items, gems, and tailor made style things. The combination of present day extravagance and conventional appeal makes Souk Al Bahar an unmistakable shopping objective, where each buy is an excursion into creativity and restrictiveness.

The Road at Etihad Pinnacles, settled inside the Jumeirah at Etihad Pinnacles complex, offers a refined shopping experience for those looking for eliteness. This store shopping road organizes a choice of worldwide and neighborhood extravagance brands, making a feel of refinement and insight.

Gastronomic Lavishness: Culinary Excursions for the Luxurious

Dubai's culinary scene reflects the city's rising into extravagance, with a gastronomic scene that takes special care of the most insightful palates. Pierchic, an overwater café settled toward the finish of its confidential wharf in the Middle Eastern Bay, encapsulates culinary lavishness. Spend significant time in fish, Pierchic offers all encompassing perspectives on the Bay and the Dubai shoreline, making an eating experience that rises above the standard to turn into an excursion into the domains of extravagance.

The Burj Al Middle Easterner takes culinary guilty pleasure higher than ever with its variety of a-list eateries. Al Mahara, a submerged café with a hypnotizing aquarium setting, epitomizes Dubai's obligation to pushing the limits of culinary development. Visitors set out on a gastronomic journey organized by eminent gourmet specialists, encompassed in a vibe that consistently mixes extravagance and debauchery.

Past the high end food encounters, Dubai embraces different culinary contributions, from lively road food markets to food celebrations that celebrate worldwide flavors. The Dubai Food Celebration, a yearly spectacle, unites Michelin-featured gourmet experts, food fans, and culinary developments, exhibiting the city's obligation to giving a different and dynamic gastronomic experience.

Diversion On easy street: Extreme Pursuits

Dubai's obligation to diversion is inseparable from excess, as the city has elite exhibitions, shows, and occasions that draw in worldwide crowds looking for unrivaled encounters. The Dubai Drama, with its dazzling plan motivated by conventional dhow sails, is a social symbol that has a different scope of exhibitions, from show and expressive dance to shows by global craftsmen. It remains as a demonstration of Dubai's devotion to encouraging an energetic expressions and diversion scene that supplements its extravagance contributions.

Worldwide Town, a yearly multicultural celebration, changes into a kaleidoscope of varieties, music, and exhibitions from around the world. This outside event highlights structures addressing various nations, each offering a novel mix of diversion, shopping, and culinary joys. Worldwide Town is a demonstration of Dubai's obligation to praising variety and giving a worldwide stage to social trade.

In the domain of sports and relaxation, Dubai's obligation to lavishness is exemplified by occasions, for example, the Dubai World Cup, one of the most extravagant horse races on the planet. Held at the Meydan Racecourse, this occasion draws in equestrian devotees, high-profile characters, and the worldwide tip top for a day of high-stakes hustling and unmatched extravagance encounters.

5.2 World-class hotels, shopping, and entertainment options.

Top notch Inns, Shopping, and Diversion: Dubai's Excessive Ternion

Dubai, with its notable horizon and visionary metropolitan turn of events, remains as a signal of extravagance, consistently mixing top notch inns, shopping, and diversion to make an excessive set of three that baits worldwide voyagers looking for the exemplification of lavishness and complexity.

Lavish Homesteads: A Pantheon of Elite Lodgings

Dubai's lodgings are not simply places of convenience; they are vivid encounters that reclassify extravagance residing. The Burj Al Bedouin, frequently proclaimed as the embodiment of luxurious cordiality, stands tall as an image of Dubai's obligation to offering unrivaled plushness. This sail-molded wonder, roosted on its own island, is frequently alluded to as the main seven-star lodging on the planet. Its extravagant insides, embellished with gold leaf and multifaceted mosaics, set up for an encounter that rises above customary thoughts of extravagance.

One more gem in Dubai's neighborliness crown is the Burj Khalifa, the world's tallest structure, which houses the extravagant Armani Inn. The upper floors of this engineering wonder offer selective homes and corporate suites, giving inhabitants and visitors stunning perspectives on the city and the Bedouin Bay. The Armani Inn mirrors the polish and complexity inseparable from the eminent design brand, making a living encounter that is however sharp as it very well might be sumptuous.

The Palm Jumeirah, a fake archipelago formed like a palm tree, has a variety of super rich retreats that reclassify ocean front lavishness. Atlantis, The Palm, with its marine-themed engineering, offers submerged suites, big name gourmet specialist eateries, and a confidential ocean side, embodying the quintessence of a selective island retreat. The Jumeirah Ocean side Lodging, with its sail-formed plan roused by the Bedouin dhow, is one more ocean front asylum that joins contemporary extravagance with unrivaled perspectives on the Middle Eastern Inlet.

Dubai's desert withdraws, for example, the Al Maha Desert Resort and Spa and the Bab Al Farces Desert Resort and Spa, offer a safe-haven of extravagance in the midst of the peaceful desert scene. Confined estates, confidential dive pools, and vivid desert encounters reclassify the idea of a retreat, furnishing visitors with a desert spring of complexity and quietness.

Retail Wonderland: Top of the line Shopping Party

Dubai's standing as a shopping heaven is unmatched, with shopping centers that are business spaces as well as extreme features of extravagance brands, planner stores, and state of the art design.

The Dubai Shopping center, one of the world's biggest shopping and diversion objections, is a microcosm of extravagance. It houses top of the line shops, including Chanel, Gucci, and Louis Vuitton, making it a famous hub for style devotees looking for the most recent patterns and extravagance manifestations. The rambling Design Road inside the shopping center is a devoted region for extravagance brands, offering a consistent mix of style and complexity.

Nearby the Dubai Shopping center is Souk Al Bahar, a cutting edge understanding of a customary Bedouin market. This shop shopping objective elements stores offering interesting high quality items, adornments, and custom style things. The combination of current extravagance and customary appeal makes Souk Al Bahar an unmistakable shopping experience, where each buy is an excursion into creativity and selectiveness.

The Road at Etihad Pinnacles, settled inside the Jumeirah at Etihad Pinnacles complex, takes care of those looking for a more close and select shopping experience. This store shopping road organizes a determination of global and neighborhood extravagance brands, making a feel of refinement and wisdom.

Past the shopping centers, Dubai's shopping experience stretches out to energetic road markets and customary souks. The Gold Souk, famous for its stunning exhibit of gold and gems, and the Flavor Souk, with its sweet-smelling flavors and conventional Center Eastern items, offer a brief look into Dubai's rich legacy while giving a sumptuous and vivid shopping climate.

Culinary Spectacle: Gastronomic Excursions for Authorities

Dubai's culinary scene is a dynamic embroidery of flavors, surfaces, and culinary craftsmanship that takes special care of the most insightful palates. Pierchic, an overwater eatery arranged toward the finish of its confidential wharf in the Middle Eastern Bay, exemplifies culinary luxury. Work in fish, Pierchic offers all encompassing perspectives on the Bay and the Dubai shore, making a feasting experience that rises above the normal to turn into an excursion into the domains of extravagance.

The Burj Al Bedouin, with its variety of elite cafés, raises eating to a work of art. Al Mahara, a submerged eatery with a hypnotizing aquarium setting, epitomizes Dubai's obligation to pushing the limits of culinary development. Visitors set out on a gastronomic journey organized by famous culinary specialists, encompassed in a feeling that consistently mixes extravagance and debauchery.

Dubai's culinary scene isn't restricted to high end food; it stretches out to dynamic road food markets and food celebrations that celebrate worldwide flavors. The Dubai Food Celebration, a yearly party, unites Michelin-featured cooks, food lovers, and culinary developments, displaying the city's obligation to giving a different and dynamic gastronomic experience.

Diversion Spectacle: A Kaleidoscope of Exhibitions

Dubai's obligation to amusement is inseparable from lavishness, as the city has elite exhibitions, shows, and occasions that draw in worldwide crowds looking for unmatched encounters. The Dubai Drama, with its staggering plan motivated by conventional dhow sails, is a social symbol that has a different scope of exhibitions, from show and artful dance to shows by worldwide specialists. It remains as a demonstration of Dubai's commitment to encouraging a lively expressions and diversion scene that supplements its extravagance contributions.

Worldwide Town, a yearly multicultural celebration, changes into a kaleidoscope of varieties, music, and exhibitions from around the world. This outside spectacle highlights structures addressing various nations, each offering an exceptional mix of diversion, shopping, and culinary enjoyments. Worldwide Town is a demonstration of Dubai's obligation to praising variety and giving a worldwide stage to social trade.

In the domain of sports and relaxation, Dubai's obligation to luxury is exemplified by occasions, for example, the Dubai World Cup, one of the most extravagant horse races on the planet. Held at the Meydan Racecourse, this occasion draws in equestrian lovers, high-profile characters, and the worldwide tip top for a day of high-stakes hustling and unrivaled extravagance encounters.

5.3 The development of Dubai as a global tourism hotspot.

The Improvement of Dubai as a Worldwide The travel industry Area of interest: A Story of Vision, Development, and Luxury

The rise of Dubai as a worldwide the travel industry area of interest is a surprising excursion that rises above the limits of customary turn of events. From its modest starting points as a little fishing and exchanging town, Dubai has changed into a stunning city that draws in huge number of guests every year. This investigation digs into the complex factors that have added to Dubai's climb as a worldwide the travel industry force to be reckoned with, incorporating visionary initiative, vital preparation, inventive foundation, and a guarantee to offering unrivaled encounters.

Visionary Administration and Key Preparation: Underpinnings of Change

At the core of Dubai's change into a worldwide the travel industry area of interest lies the visionary initiative of rulers and a pledge to key arranging opposes traditional standards. Sheik Rashid container Saeed Al Maktoum, the dad of current Dubai, established the groundwork for the city's advancement during the twentieth hundred years. His visionary methodology zeroed in on broadening the economy past oil, expecting the possible decay of oil holds.

The defining moment accompanied the rising of Sheik Mohammed receptacle Rashid Al Maktoum to control in 2006.

Under his administration, Dubai embraced an aggressive vision for what was to come epitomized in drives like Vision 2020 and the Dubai The travel industry Methodology. Vision 2020 illustrated a guide for Dubai to turn into a worldwide center point for the travel industry, exchange, and money. The procedure underscored the significance of the travel industry as a vital driver of monetary development, meaning to draw in 20 million yearly guests by 2020.

Vital arranging was manifest in the foundation of key areas, like land, flying, and cordiality, each assuming a critical part in molding Dubai's travel industry scene. The Dubai The travel industry Methodology included joint efforts between government substances, confidential areas, and worldwide accomplices to make a far reaching and supportable way to deal with the travel industry improvement.

Imaginative Framework: Forming the City Representing things to come

Dubai's horizon, with its notable high rises, is a demonstration of the city's obligation to development in framework. The advancement of milestones like the Burj Khalifa, the world's tallest structure, and the Palm Jumeirah, a fake archipelago, reshaped the cityscape, making attractions that draw guests from across the globe.

The Burj Khalifa, remaining at north of 828 meters, is in excess of a wonder of designing; it's an image of Dubai's assurance to arrive at new levels. Its perception decks give all encompassing perspectives on the city, the desert, and the shore, offering a stunning encounter that encapsulates Dubai's obligation to giving unrivaled attractions.

The Palm Jumeirah, considered as a man-made island molded like a palm tree, is a demonstration of Dubai's capacity to reshape its geology for both private and touristic purposes. Facilitating extravagance resorts, upscale homes, and diversion choices, the Palm Jumeirah has turned into an image of lavishness and development.

The Dubai Shopping center, one of the world's biggest shopping and amusement objections, is a vital area of the city's creative framework. Past its sheer size and retail contributions, the shopping center highlights attractions like the Dubai Aquarium and Submerged Zoo, displaying Dubai's capacity to incorporate amusement consistently into its metropolitan texture.

Excessive Hotels and Friendliness: Making Remarkable Encounters

Dubai's change into a worldwide the travel industry area of interest is naturally attached to its capacity to offer elite neighborliness and extreme hotels. The Burj Al Bedouin, frequently hailed as the world's just seven-star inn, is a design wonder that has turned into a famous image of extravagance. Its sail-molded outline and lavish insides give an encounter that goes past traditional convenience, setting the norm for top of the line neighborliness.

Atlantis, The Palm, arranged on the Palm Jumeirah, is one more demonstration of Dubai's obligation to creating remarkable encounters. With submerged suites, a waterpark, superstar culinary expert cafés, and a confidential ocean side, Atlantis offers a vivid retreat that consolidates extravagance with diversion.

Dubai's desert resorts, for example, the Al Maha Desert Resort and Spa and the Bab Al Hoaxes Desert Resort and Spa, grandstand the city's capacity to make desert gardens of serenity in the midst of the huge desert scene. These hotels offer a mix of withdrawal, extravagance, and vivid desert encounters, taking care of an insightful customer base looking for a one of a kind and liberal retreat.

The improvement of excessive hotels and friendliness foundations is supplemented by a commitment to offering customized types of assistance. Dubai's cordiality industry has embraced a culture of greatness, with an emphasis on expecting and surpassing the assumptions for guests. From rich facilities to top notch food encounters and health contributions, Dubai's inns and resorts are intended to make a comprehensive and liberal experience.

Various Attractions: Past High rises and Shopping centers

While Dubai is frequently connected with its notable high rises and extravagance shopping centers, the city has expanded its attractions to take special care of a wide range of interests. Dubai's social region, moored by the Dubai Drama, the Dubai Exhibition hall, and the Alserkal Road expressions locale, mirrors a promise to displaying the city's rich legacy and encouraging an energetic expressions and culture scene.

Worldwide Town, a yearly multicultural celebration, changes into a powerful commercial center where guests can encounter the way of life of north of 80 nations. The occasion highlights structures, exhibitions, and culinary enjoyments, making a worldwide stage for social trade and festivity.

Dubai's obligation to giving assorted attractions stretches out to open air encounters. The Dubai Supernatural occurrence Nursery, a botanical event highlighting elaborate presentations of roses and plants, and the Dubai Desert Preservation Hold, a safeguarded region that offers desert encounters and natural life experiences, exhibit the city's capacity to offer a large number of outside exercises.

Experience the travel industry has additionally acquired conspicuousness in Dubai, with attractions like Ski Dubai, an indoor ski resort in the Shopping center of the Emirates, and the XLine Dubai Marina, one of the world's longest metropolitan ziplines. These contributions take special care of daredevils and adrenaline fans, adding a powerful aspect to Dubai's travel industry scene.

Worldwide Occasions and Celebrations: Exhibiting Dubai on the World Stage

Dubai's rise as a worldwide the travel industry area of interest is complemented by its job as a host for significant global occasions and celebrations. The city has situated itself as a scene for business gatherings, sports contests, and social celebrations, drawing guests from around the world.

Exhibition 2020, initially planned for 2020 however deferred to 2021 because of worldwide conditions, embodies Dubai's desire to have a worldwide occasion that rises above conventional limits. The exhibition intends to unite countries, organizations, and trailblazers to feature answers for worldwide difficulties and celebrate human creativity.

The Dubai Shopping Celebration, a yearly occasion that changes the city into a customer's heaven, draws in huge number of guests with its advancements, limits, and diversion contributions. The celebration has turned into a worldwide peculiarity, adding to Dubai's standing as a center for retail the travel industry.

Dubai's facilitating of major games, including the Dubai Tennis Titles, the Dubai World Cup, and the DP World Visit Title, upgrades its status as an objective for sports devotees. These occasions draw in worldwide competitors as well as position Dubai as a worldwide games center point.

Availability and Openness: Crossing over Mainlands

Dubai's essential area and obligation to network play had a significant impact in its change into a worldwide the travel industry area of interest. The city's leader transporter, Emirates Aircrafts, has arisen as one of the world's driving carriers, interfacing Dubai to more than 150 objections across six mainlands. The cutting edge Dubai Global Air terminal fills in as a significant travel center point, working with consistent travel for guests from around the world.

The Dubai Voyage Terminal, situated in the core of the city, has additionally improved Dubai's openness for journey lovers. The terminal fills in as a port of call for significant voyage lines, offering travelers the valuable chance to investigate Dubai's attractions and experience its cordiality.

Manageability Drives: Forming the Fate of The travel industry

As Dubai keeps on developing as a worldwide the travel industry area of interest, manageability has turned into a key concentration. The city has carried out different drives to limit its ecological effect and advance dependable the travel industry. The Dubai Feasible The travel industry (DST) drive expects to make Dubai a main supportable the travel industry objective, zeroing in on regions like energy effectiveness, squander decrease, and local area commitment.

Dubai's obligation to maintainability is clear in projects like the Mohammed canister Rashid Al Maktoum Sun based Park, perhaps of the biggest sun oriented park on the planet. The recreation area adds to Dubai's objective of inferring 75% of its energy from clean sources by 2050, lining up with worldwide endeavors to battle environmental change.

Green structure drives, for example, the Dubai Green Structure Guidelines and Particulars, highlight the city's obligation to harmless to the ecosystem development rehearses. The Dubai Water Channel project, which changed a noteworthy stream into a lively waterfront, coordinates economical plan standards to improve water protection and biodiversity.

Chapter 6

"Connecting Continents: Transportation Hub"

Interfacing Mainlands: Dubai's Ascent as a Transportation Center

In the core of the Bedouin Promontory, Dubai has arisen as a worldwide transportation center point, associating mainlands and working with the consistent development of individuals and merchandise. This story investigates the essential variables, imaginative framework, and visionary arranging that have pushed Dubai into a critical job in worldwide transportation, making it a junction where East meets West, and North meets South.

Key Area: Crossing over East and West

Dubai's rising as a transportation center is complicatedly connected to its vital geological area. Arranged at the intersection of Asia, Europe, and Africa, Dubai fills in as a characteristic scaffold between the East and the West, giving an essential issue to global travel and exchange. This essential situating has been an impetus for the city's development, changing it into an indispensable connection that interfaces mainlands.

Dubai's area along the noteworthy shipping lanes that spread over the Middle Eastern Promontory plays had a significant impact in its turn of events. The city's old roots as a general store have developed into a cutting edge city that use its essential situation to work with worldwide network. As shipping lanes moved from ocean to air, Dubai adjusted to turn into a critical center for both sea and flying transportation.

Air Availability: Emirates Carriers and Dubai Worldwide Air terminal

At the core of Dubai's prosperity as an air transportation center point is Emirates Aircrafts, the lead transporter of the Unified Bedouin Emirates. Laid out in 1985, Emirates has developed into one of the world's biggest and most perceived carriers, associating Dubai to more than 150 objections across six landmasses. The aircraft's obligation to greatness, advancement, and client care has set new norms in the flying business.

Dubai Global Air terminal (DXB) remains as a demonstration of the city's devotion to air network. Since opening in 1960, DXB has developed into one of the most active air terminals worldwide, filling in as a significant travel center point for a large number of travelers every year. Its cutting edge offices, broad flight organization, and vital area have made it a favored visit for explorers on the way to different objections.

DXB's Concourse A, committed to Emirates Carriers, epitomizes the city's obligation to giving a top notch travel insight. With sumptuous parlors, obligation free shopping, and proficient administrations, Concourse A mirrors Dubai's goal to offer something beyond a travel point however an objective inside itself.

Flying Greatness: Dubai World Focal and Al Maktoum Global Air terminal

To oblige the steadily expanding interest for air travel, Dubai has extended its avionics foundation with the advancement of Dubai World Focal (DWC) and Al Maktoum Global Air terminal. DWC, planned as a multi-modular strategies stage, intends to upgrade Dubai's situation as a worldwide freight center point, consistently coordinating air, ocean, and land transport.

Al Maktoum Global Air terminal, arranged inside Dubai World Focal, addresses the following stage in Dubai's flight advancement. Upon fruition, it is normal to turn into the world's biggest air terminal, with the ability to every year deal with north of 220 million travelers. This aggressive undertaking mirrors Dubai's forward-looking way to deal with fulfilling the needs of a quickly developing flight industry.

Sea Network: Jebel Ali Port and Mina Rashid

Dubai's sea network is moored by Jebel Ali Port, one of the world's biggest and most active compartment ports. Decisively situated on the edge of the Bedouin Bay, Jebel Ali Port has turned into a crucial connection in worldwide shipping lanes, working with the development of products between Asia, Europe, and Africa.

Its cutting edge offices, productive tasks, and network to significant transportation paths have pushed it into an oceanic force to be reckoned with.

Jebel Ali Port's free zone, Jebel Ali Free Zone (JAFZA), further upgrades Dubai's allure as a strategies and exchanging center point. JAFZA gives a business-accommodating climate to organizations participated in exchange, assembling, and planned operations, drawing in global organizations looking for an essential base in the Center East.

Mina Rashid, Dubai's notable port, has been changed into a cutting edge voyage terminal, inviting extravagance luxury ships from around the world. The terminal, with its mix of sea legacy and contemporary offices, mirrors Dubai's obligation to enhancing its contributions and turning into an objective for oceanic the travel industry.

Land Network: Streets and Framework

Dubai's obligation to exhaustive land availability is apparent in its broad street organizations and creative framework projects. The city's streets and parkways work with effective development inside the emirate and interface Dubai to adjoining locales. The Sheik Zayed Street, a significant conduit that goes through the core of Dubai, fills in as a life saver for workers and organizations the same.

The Dubai Metro, sent off in 2009, remains as a worldview of development in metropolitan transportation. As one of the world's most developed and current metro frameworks, it gives a feasible and effective method of transportation for occupants and guests. The development of the metro network highlights Dubai's obligation to upgrading public transportation and decreasing dependence on confidential vehicles.

Furthermore, the improvement of famous designs like the Dubai Water Channel, a man-made trench that winds through the city, and the Dubai River Harbor, a waterfront advancement, exhibit Dubai's obligation to coordinating water transport into its metropolitan texture. Water taxicabs and ships employ the waters, offering elective and picturesque methods of transportation.

Exhibition 2020: A Worldwide Intermingling

Dubai's impending Exhibition 2020, in spite of the fact that deferred to 2021, addresses a stupendous occasion that will additionally raise the city's status as a world-wide transportation center point. The Exhibition is supposed to draw in large number of guests from around the world, uniting countries, organizations, and pioneers to grandstand answers for worldwide difficulties. Dubai's capacity to host such a uber occasion mirrors its top notch foundation, hierarchical ability, and obligation to being a focal hub in the worldwide organization.

Maintainability in Transportation: Molding What's to come

As Dubai positions itself for the future, maintainability in transportation has turned into a key concentration. The city's drives incorporate the mix of electric and cross breed vehicles into its public transportation armada, the improvement of cycling tracks, and interests in brilliant transportation frameworks. Dubai means to diminish its carbon impression, mitigate gridlock, and advance harmless to the ecosystem methods of transport.

6.1 Dubai's strategic importance in global transportation.

Dubai's Essential Significance in Worldwide Transportation: A Juncture of Exchange, Development, and Network

Dubai's essential significance in worldwide transportation is a story that unfurls against the background of a little fishing town developing into a powerful city at the junction of mainlands. In the core of the Center East, Dubai has risen above its unassuming beginnings to turn into a urgent center that associates East to West as well as assumes an extraordinary part in forming worldwide exchange, encouraging development, and rethinking the principles of network.

Exchange Nexus: Working with Worldwide Trade

Dubai's essential importance in worldwide transportation is well established in its verifiable job as an exchange nexus. The city's topographical area at the junction of Asia, Europe, and Africa has situated it as a characteristic gathering point for different societies, merchandise, and thoughts. By and large, Dubai's port was a basic hub in the oceanic Silk Street, working with exchange between the East and the West. Today, this heritage go on as Dubai remains as a lively center point for worldwide business.

Jebel Ali Port, one of the world's biggest and most active holder ports, is the key part of Dubai's oceanic exchange. Its essential area on the Bedouin Inlet permits simple admittance to significant delivery courses, making it an ideal parcel point for merchandise moving between Asia, Europe, and Africa. The port's free zone, Jebel Ali Free Zone (JAFZA), further upgrades Dubai's exchange capacities by furnishing organizations with an essential base for assembling, dissemination, and coordinated operations.

The Dubai Sea City, an aggressive venture pointed toward uniting sea related organizations, mirrors Dubai's obligation to reinforcing its situation as a worldwide exchange center. This city inside a city is intended to house delivering organizations, oceanic specialist co-ops, and subordinate enterprises, making a synergistic environment that drives Dubai to the very front of the sea exchange scene.

Notwithstanding sea exchange, Dubai has decisively enhanced its transportation portfolio to incorporate air and land network, guaranteeing an exhaustive and coordinated way to deal with worldwide exchange.

The city's obligation to improving exchange is embodied in its aggressive Dubai Silk Street drive, which looks to use Dubai's essential area to renew the noteworthy Silk Street shipping lanes through a multimodal transportation organization.

Aviation Aspirations: Lifting Air Network

Dubai's introduction to the airplane business, especially through Emirates Carriers, has been a unique advantage in the domain of worldwide air transportation. Laid out in 1985, Emirates has turned into an image of greatness and development in the flight area. Its broad organization of flights interfacing Dubai to more than 150 objections has worked with traveler travel as well as made the city a worldwide freight center.

Dubai Worldwide Air terminal (DXB) fills in as the operational hub for Emirates and a urgent component in the city's worldwide network. As quite possibly of the most active air terminal on the planet, DXB handles a huge number of travelers and lots of freight yearly. The air terminal's cutting edge framework, effective tasks, and key area have changed it into a key travel point for voyagers and a passage for merchandise getting across landmasses.

The Dubai World Focal (DWC) and Al Maktoum Global Air terminal address Dubai's visionary way to deal with fulfilling the needs of a quickly developing flight industry. As DWC forms into a multi-modular operations stage, reinforcing Dubai's situation in worldwide air transportation is ready. Al Maktoum Global Air terminal, upon fulfillment, is supposed to turn into the world's biggest air terminal, a demonstration of Dubai's obligation to setting new benchmarks in the flying area.

Emirates SkyCargo, the airship cargo division of Emirates, assumes an essential part in Dubai's worldwide transportation procedure. By moving merchandise going from perishables to high-esteem wares, Emirates SkyCargo adds to Dubai's remaining as a strategic center that interfaces makers and buyers around the world.

Land Network: Streets, Rail, and Then some

Dubai's essential significance isn't restricted to air and ocean; the city has put fundamentally in land transportation to make a consistent organization that upgrades network inside the district and then some. The Sheik Zayed Street, a significant blood vessel thruway, goes through the core of Dubai, interfacing the emirate to adjoining states and encouraging monetary mix.

The Dubai Metro, sent off in 2009, has reformed metropolitan transportation, offering a practical and proficient method for driving inside the city. Its extension, including the presentation of new lines and the joining of shrewd innovations, highlights Dubai's obligation to exhaustive and current land transportation.

Development in land network stretches out to visionary tasks like the Hyperloop, a fast transportation framework that means to upset intercity travel. With proposed courses associating Dubai to other significant urban communities in the locale, the Hyperloop addresses the city's obligation to pushing the limits of transportation innovation.

Dubai's obligation to advancement in land network reaches out past customary methods of transport. The Dubai Water Trench, a man-made stream that moves through the city, coordinates water transport into the metropolitan texture. Water taxicabs and ships give an elective method of movement as well as add to Dubai's obligation to making a supportable and various transportation environment.

Exhibition 2020: A Worldwide Feature of Network

Dubai's essential significance in worldwide transportation is set to arrive at new levels with the facilitating of Exhibition 2020, a worldwide occasion that will draw in huge number of guests, organizations, and trend-setters from around the world. The Exhibition site is intended to be a model of network, including cutting edge framework, shrewd transportation arrangements, and a stage for global coordinated effort.

The Exhibition's subject, "Interfacing Psyches, Making What's in store," mirrors Dubai's desire to grandstand the city as a worldwide center that encourages network, development, and joint effort. The occasion isn't just a chance for Dubai to feature its accomplishments in transportation yet in addition a stage to shape the eventual fate of worldwide network through discourse and trade.

Maintainability in Transportation: A Forward-Looking Methodology

Dubai's essential significance in worldwide transportation isn't just about actual network yet additionally about forming the future with a manageable and forward-looking methodology. The city's obligation to maintainability is obvious in drives like the combination of electric and half and half vehicles into public transportation, the improvement of cycling tracks, and interests in savvy transportation frameworks.

The Dubai Independent Transportation Procedure, sent off in 2017, expects to change 25% of the complete transportation in Dubai to independent mode by 2030. This forward-looking methodology mirrors Dubai's assurance to embrace state of the art advancements that improve proficiency, diminish discharges, and reclassify the scene of metropolitan transportation.

The city's obligation to maintainability is additionally highlighted by the Mohammed receptacle Rashid Al Maktoum Sun based Park, perhaps of the biggest sun oriented park on the planet. As Dubai moves towards a more economical energy future, the transportation area assumes an essential part in adding to the city's aggressive ecological objectives.

6.2 The evolution of aviation with Dubai International Airport.

The Development of Flying with Dubai Worldwide Air terminal: A Heavenward Rising

Dubai Global Air terminal (DXB), settled at the junction of mainlands and societies, has arisen as an image of Dubai's tenacious quest for greatness in the flight business. The story of Dubai's flying development is complicatedly woven into the texture of this clamoring air terminal, mirroring the city's visionary methodology, key preparation, and steady obligation to turning into a worldwide flight force to be reckoned with.

Beginning and Development: From Humble Starting points to Worldwide Noticeable quality

Dubai Global Air terminal follows its underlying foundations back to the 1960s when the principal terminal was developed to take special care of the humble air travel requests of the time. By then, Dubai was a little emirate with desires of development, and the air terminal was a demonstration of its prescience. Throughout the long term, as Dubai's economy enhanced and the city turned into a center point for exchange and trade, the interest for air travel flooded, making way for the air terminal's extension.

The defining moment in Dubai's aeronautics direction came in 1985 with the foundation of Emirates Aircrafts. The state-claimed transporter left on an excursion to change DXB into a significant worldwide center, denoting the start of an organization that would move both the carrier and the air terminal to phenomenal levels. Emirates' essential vision, combined with Dubai's obligation to giving elite framework, established the groundwork for the air terminal's advancement.

Vital Area and Network: A Center really taking shape

Dubai's topographical area, decisively situated between the East and the West, assumed an essential part in molding the air terminal's fate. DXB turned into a characteristic visit for long stretch flights, making a center point that associated landmasses and worked with consistent travel between Europe, Asia, Africa, and then some. This upper hand, combined with a ground breaking initiative, situated DXB as a center point that rose above local importance.

Emirates' rise as a worldwide transporter further enhanced DXB's network. The carrier's broad organization, with Dubai as its focal center point, changed the air terminal into a nexus where travelers could consistently travel between different objections. Dubai's open skies strategy, permitting carriers from around the world to work uninhibitedly, added to the air terminal's standing as a blend of societies and a door to the world.

Terminal Greatness: Engineering Wonders and Traveler Experience

The compositional ability of DXB's terminals mirrors Dubai's obligation to setting new principles in air terminal plan and traveler experience. Terminal 1, portrayed by its famous vault, was a spearheading structure that mixed present day feel with conventional Arabic plan components. Ensuing terminals, including the rambling Terminal 3 committed to Emirates, proceeded with this pattern of design advancement.

Terminal 3 stands as one of the biggest air terminal terminals internationally and is a demonstration of Dubai's desire to make an unmatched traveler experience. It houses Emirates as well as obliges other worldwide transporters. The terminal's cutting edge offices, sweeping obligation free shopping, and lavish parlors rethink the idea of air terminal friendliness. The sheer scale and extravagance of Terminal 3 highlight Dubai's obligation to making each explorer's excursion through the city an involvement with itself.

DXB's Concourse A, a committed office for Emirates' A380 armada, epitomizes Dubai's emphasis on offering premium types of assistance. The concourse flaunts selective parlors, top notch food choices, and a degree of solace that lines up with the city's standing for extravagance. This obligation to traveler solace has procured DXB various honors, including acknowledgment as one of the world's most active air terminals while keeping up with high traveler fulfillment levels.

Functional Greatness: Overseeing Development and Proficiency

The development of DXB didn't come without its difficulties, especially in dealing with the remarkable development in air traffic. The air terminal's runways, runways, and terminals went through persistent extensions and moves up to oblige the rising number of flights and travelers. Dubai's capacity to consistently deal with this development while keeping up with functional proficiency is a demonstration of its versatile preparation and obligation to greatness.

The execution of state of the art advancements further improved DXB's functional capacities. From mechanized registration booths to cutting edge things taking care of frameworks, Dubai utilized development to smooth out processes and furnish travelers with a problem free encounter. The emphasis on innovation stretched out to aviation authority and route frameworks, guaranteeing that DXB stayed at the very front of avionics progressions.

Dubai's obligation to functional greatness is typified by its assurance to develop notwithstanding difficulties. For example, during the Coronavirus pandemic, DXB executed severe wellbeing and security measures, including progressed disinfection processes, contactless administrations, and best in class warm screening. This proactive methodology guaranteed the security of travelers as well as shown Dubai's strength and flexibility even with exceptional difficulties.

Freight Center point: Working with Worldwide Exchange

Past its job as a traveler center, DXB has turned into a fundamental passage for the worldwide development of freight. Emirates SkyCargo, the airship cargo division of Emirates Carriers, uses DXB's broad freight offices to move products going from perishables to high-esteem wares. The air terminal's freight terminals and committed vessel airplane add to Dubai's remaining as a calculated stalwart that interfaces makers and shoppers around the world.

Dubai's emphasis on turning into a worldwide planned operations and exchanging center point is reflected in drives, for example, the Dubai Silk Street, which means to use the city's essential area to renew noteworthy shipping lanes. The reconciliation of air freight administrations at DXB with oceanic and land-based coordinated operations further positions Dubai as a focal hub in the worldwide store network.

What's to come: Growing Skylines with Dubai World Focal

As Dubai Global Air terminal keeps on being a clamoring very busy place, the city has focused on the future with Dubai World Focal (DWC). Considered as a multi-modular strategies stage, DWC is intended to supplement DXB's tasks and improve Dubai's situation as a worldwide transportation center. With plans for extra runways, traveler terminals, and freight offices, DWC is ready to assume an essential part in molding the following period of Dubai's flying development.

Al Maktoum Worldwide Air terminal, arranged inside DWC, addresses the following outskirts in Dubai's aeronautics aspirations. Once finished, outperforming DXB in size and limit, hardening Dubai's status as a worldwide flying giant is normal. The air terminal's essential area close to Jebel Ali Port and its joining with planned operations and free zone offices line up with Dubai's all-encompassing vision of consistent availability across air, ocean, and land.

6.3 Land and sea connectivity through advanced infrastructure.

Land and Ocean Availability through Cutting edge Framework: Dubai's Unmatched Incorporation

In the core of the Middle Eastern Promontory, where the huge desert meets the shining waters of the Bedouin Bay, Dubai has arisen as a worldwide symbol of network, flawlessly mixing progressed foundation to work with land and ocean transport. The narrative of Dubai's territory and ocean network is one of visionary preparation, imaginative undertakings, and a promise to making a coordinated transportation biological system that rises above customary limits.

Land Network: Streets as Helps

Dubai's obligation to thorough land availability is distinctively reflected in its broad street organization, with the Sheik Zayed Street filling in as the foundation of the city's transportation framework.

Extending from the boundary with Abu Dhabi toward the northern emirates, this eight-path expressway is a demonstration of Dubai's commitment to making a consistent connection between various districts of the Unified Middle Easterner Emirates (UAE).

The Sheik Zayed Street isn't just a lane; a help works with the development of individuals and merchandise, interfacing key regions inside Dubai and filling in as the essential corridor for suburbanites and organizations. The street is fixed with notable high rises, mirroring the city's horizon and filling in as a visual demonstration of Dubai's quick urbanization and financial development.

Dubai's obligation to greatness in street framework reaches out past the Sheik Zayed Street. The city has put resources into various flyovers, underpasses, and street extensions to mitigate gridlock and improve availability. The Dubai Trench, a man-made stream that slices through the city, has not just added a beautiful component to the metropolitan scene yet has likewise prompted the improvement of new streets and scaffolds, further coordinating area transportation.

The Dubai Metro, presented in 2009, remains as a worldview of development in metropolitan transportation. As one of the world's most developed and present day metro frameworks, it gives a supportable and proficient method for driving for inhabitants and guests the same. The metro's development plans, including new lines and stations, highlight Dubai's obligation to improving public transportation and lessening dependence on confidential vehicles.

Furthermore, Dubai has embraced arising advances in land network. The city has been at the front of testing and carrying out independent and electric vehicles, flagging a future where shrewd and manageable transportation frameworks will assume a crucial part in metropolitan portability.

Waterfront Advancement: Changing the Coastline

Dubai's shoreline, extending along the Middle Eastern Bay, has been a material for extraordinary tasks that coordinate ocean transport into the city's framework. The Dubai Spring, a noteworthy stream that isolates the city into two principal locale — Deira and Bramble Dubai — has been a point of convergence of Dubai's sea legacy. Throughout the long term, the river has seen an exceptional change, developing from a conventional exchanging port to a cutting edge and lively waterfront.

The Dubai Water Channel, a pivotal task introduced in 2016, has reclassified Dubai's waterfront experience. This counterfeit trench reaches out from the Stream in Old Dubai to the Middle Eastern Bay, making another association between the noteworthy regions and the advanced improvements of the city. Fixed with passerby ways, cycling tracks, and green spaces, the trench incorporates flawlessly into the metropolitan texture, empowering elective methods of transportation and cultivating a feeling of local area commitment.

Past the trench, Dubai's obligation to waterfront advancement is obvious in projects like the Dubai Marina and Jumeirah Ocean side Home (JBR). These beach front improvements offer sumptuous private and business spaces as well as add to establishing a powerful metropolitan climate where ocean transport, including water cabs and ships, turns into an indispensable piece of the transportation scene.

Oceanic Network: Jebel Ali Port and Mina Rashid

Dubai's oceanic network is secured by Jebel Ali Port, one of the world's biggest and most active compartment ports. Arranged on the southwestern edges of the city,

Jebel Ali Port has turned into a fundamental connection in worldwide shipping lanes, working with the development of merchandise between Asia, Europe, and Africa. Its essential area on the edge of the Middle Eastern Bay positions it as an entryway for transportation lines entering the locale.

The port's free zone, Jebel Ali Free Zone (JAFZA), further upgrades Dubai's allure as a coordinated operations and exchanging center point. JAFZA gives a business-accommodating climate to organizations participated in exchange, assembling, and planned operations, drawing in global organizations looking for an essential base in the Center East.

Mina Rashid, Dubai's memorable port, has been changed into a cutting edge journey terminal, inviting extravagance luxury ships from around the world. The terminal, with its mix of oceanic legacy and contemporary offices, mirrors Dubai's obligation to broadening its contributions and turning into an objective for sea the travel industry.

Dubai Voyage Terminal, situated at Mina Rashid, fills in as a port of call for significant journey lines, offering travelers the chance to investigate Dubai's attractions and experience its cordiality. The terminal's essential area close to the downtown area guarantees that journey guests can undoubtedly get to Dubai's milestones and add to the city's dynamic the travel industry area.

Development in Transportation Centers: Al Maktoum Worldwide Air terminal

While Dubai Global Air terminal (DXB) has been a vital participant in air transportation, the city's vision for what's to come incorporates the development of Al Maktoum Global Air terminal, arranged inside Dubai World Focal (DWC). Imagined as the world's biggest air terminal upon fruition, Al Maktoum Global Air terminal addresses a groundbreaking task that incorporates air, ocean, and land transport on an extraordinary scale.

DWC is planned as a multi-modular coordinated operations stage, pointed toward improving Dubai's situation as a worldwide freight center. The air terminal's essential area close to Jebel Ali Port and its consistent mix with street and rail networks make a calculated environment that works with the effective development of products between air, ocean, and land.

The improvement of Al Maktoum Global Air terminal lines up with Dubai's more extensive desires to make an all encompassing transportation center point. With plans for extra runways, traveler terminals, and freight offices, DWC is ready to reclassify the city's network, offering an extensive and interconnected stage for worldwide exchange and travel.

Savvy City Drives: Spearheading Network

Dubai's obligation to cutting edge foundation and network is additionally exemplified by its drives as a shrewd city. The coordination of savvy advances, including clever traffic the executives frameworks, independent vehicles, and information investigation, upgrades the productivity of land transportation. Dubai's brilliant city vision means to make an interconnected organization that streamlines traffic stream, diminishes clog, and gives constant data to workers.

The Streets and Transport Authority (RTA) in Dubai has been at the front of executing shrewd arrangements. From the acquaintance of savvy stopping frameworks with the joining of brilliant installment choices in open transportation, the RTA's drives highlight Dubai's obligation to saddling innovation for a consistent and associated metropolitan experience.

Supportability and the Fate of Network

Dubai's attention on supportability stretches out to its transportation framework. The city has carried out drives to lessen fossil fuel byproducts, advance energy effectiveness, and energize the utilization of harmless to the ecosystem methods of transport. The Dubai Independent Transportation Methodology, sent off in 2017, means to change a critical piece of the city's transportation to independent mode by 2030, adding to decreased clog and emanations.

The Dubai Metro, with its accentuation on electrically fueled trains and energy-proficient advances, epitomizes the city's obligation to manageable metropolitan transportation. Furthermore, the Dubai Water Channel project integrates reasonable plan standards to upgrade water protection and biodiversity, displaying how huge scope foundation undertakings can line up with ecological contemplations.

Dubai's commitment to manageability is further obvious in projects like the Mohammed container Rashid Al Maktoum Sun based Park, perhaps of the biggest sun oriented park on the planet. As Dubai moves towards a more supportable energy future, the transportation area assumes a urgent part in adding to the city's aggressive ecological objectives.

Chapter 7

"Innovation in Education and Research"

Advancement in Training and Exploration: Dubai's Mission for Information Greatness

In the rambling city of Dubai, in the midst of the glimmering high rises and social milestones, a quiet unrest is in progress in the domain of schooling and exploration. The city, once known fundamentally for its financial ability and compositional wonders, has decisively situated itself as a center point for information and development. This change is described by a guarantee to encouraging a culture of picking up, spearheading research drives, and embracing state of the art innovations to move training into what's in store.

Training as a Foundation: Underpinnings of Information

Dubai's excursion toward turning into an instructive force to be reckoned with can be followed back to the foundation of the Dubai Information Town in 2003. This free zone was considered as a committed locale for instructive establishments and preparing focuses, giving a helpful climate to information scattering and abilities improvement. From that point forward, Dubai has reliably put resources into instruction, remembering it as a foundation for cultural advancement and feasible turn of events.

One of the spearheading organizations in this instructive scene is the Mohammed receptacle Rashid Al Maktoum Establishment, established in 2007 with the mission to engage people in the future through schooling. The establishment plays had a significant impact in molding instructive strategies, supporting exploration, and encouraging a culture of development in learning. Its drives range from grant projects to the foundation of examination focuses, making a powerful starting point for information securing and spread.

Scholarly Greatness: Driving Establishments and Global Organizations

Dubai's obligation to scholarly greatness is exemplified by the foundation and development of top notch instructive establishments inside its nation. The Higher

Schools of Innovation (HCT) and Zayed College, among others, have been instrumental in giving top notch advanced education to understudies, furnishing them with the abilities and information expected to flourish in a quickly developing worldwide scene.

Global organizations play had a urgent impact in lifting the scholastic norms in Dubai. The city has drawn in eminent colleges from around the world, laying out neighborhood grounds and offering a different scope of projects. These organizations not just carry worldwide points of view to Dubai's schooling scene yet in addition set out open doors for understudies to draw in with driving researchers, specialists, and industry specialists.

The Dubai Worldwide Scholarly City (DIAC), laid out in 2007, remains as a demonstration of the city's obligation to turning into territorial and worldwide schooling center. DIAC gives a cooperative biological system where colleges, research focuses, and scholastic foundations coincide, encouraging interdisciplinary coordinated efforts and information trade. Its job as an impetus for instructive development is reflected in the different scope of projects and trains presented by its part foundations.

Innovative work: Supporting a Culture of Development

Dubai's introduction to innovative work denotes a change in outlook in the city's way to deal with information creation. The Dubai Exploration and Development Culmination, started by the Dubai Future Establishment, fills in as a yearly stage for scientists, scholastics, and pioneers to share bits of knowledge, exhibit forward leaps, and examine the fate of examination in the city. This highest point highlights Dubai's obligation to encouraging a culture of development and situating itself at the very front of worldwide exploration tries.

The Dubai Innovative work Community (DRDC), laid out in 2016, addresses a critical stage toward solidifying research endeavors in the city. With an emphasis on key areas like medical services, energy, and man-made reasoning, the middle teams up with neighborhood and global accomplices to drive development and address squeezing difficulties. The DRDC's drives range from financing rescarch undertakings to giving cutting edge research foundation, establishing a climate helpful for earth shattering disclosures.

Dubai's obligation to investigate stretches out past customary scholarly settings. The Dubai Future Establishment's Gallery Representing things to come, a visionary task set to open its entryways in 2023, means to be a middle for development and a stage for state of the art research. The historical center will act as a center where researchers, specialists, and creatives can meet up to investigate arising innovations, try different things with groundbreaking thoughts, and add to molding what's in store.

Innovation in Training: A Computerized Upheaval

Dubai's journey for information greatness is firmly entwined with its hug of innovation in training. The Brilliant Dubai Schooling drive, sent off in 2017, tries to use computerized advances to improve the opportunity for growth for understudies across the city. The drive centers around consolidating shrewd learning stages, virtual homerooms, and inventive helping philosophies to get ready understudies for the difficulties of the advanced age.

One of the vital mainstays of this computerized upheaval is the Mohammed canister Rashid Brilliant Learning System, which furnishes understudies with computerized gadgets, intuitive learning materials, and admittance to a huge vault of instructive assets. By coordinating innovation into study halls, Dubai plans to establish a dynamic and intelligent learning climate that encourages innovativeness, decisive reasoning, and computerized proficiency.

Dubai's obligation to innovation in schooling is additionally apparent in drives like the Mohammed container Rashid Drive for Worldwide Flourishing. Sent off as a team with the Massachusetts Establishment of Innovation (MIT), the drive outfits the force of development to address worldwide difficulties. By advancing a culture of social development and offering help to trend-setters and business people, Dubai looks to add to the worldwide information biological system.

Business and Advancement: From Homeroom to Meeting room

Dubai's instructive scene reaches out past conventional learning conditions to develop business venture and advancement. The Dubai Future Institute, sent off by the Dubai Future Establishment, fills in as a stage for consistent mastering and expertise improvement. Through a scope of projects, studios, and courses, the institute furnishes people with the information and abilities expected to explore the intricacies representing things to come.

The incorporation of advancement and business venture into instruction is additionally exemplified by drives like the Mohammed container Rashid Development Asset. This asset offers monetary help to imaginative tasks and new companies, cultivating a culture of business venture and empowering people to change their thoughts into effective arrangements.

Dubai's obligation to sustaining a culture of development is likewise obvious in the foundation of free zones committed to explicit enterprises, for example, Dubai Web City and Dubai Information Park. These zones make environments where new businesses, innovation organizations, and research foundations can team up, share thoughts, and add to the city's situation as a worldwide development center.

Worldwide Coordinated efforts: Forming the Future Together

Dubai's excursion toward information greatness is certainly not a lone undertaking; it is set apart by broad joint efforts with worldwide accomplices. The city has effectively looked to draw in driving scientists, researchers, and specialists from around the world, cultivating a climate where various viewpoints join to address complex difficulties.

The Dubai Future Gas pedals program, sent off by the Dubai Future Establishment, embodies this cooperative soul. The program unites government substances and inventive organizations to co-make answers for difficulties looked by the public area. By working with associations between government associations and innovation trend-setters, Dubai endeavors to situate itself as a testbed for state of the art arrangements with worldwide importance.

Furthermore, Dubai's worldwide viewpoint is reflected in drives like the Dubai Future Gathering for Philanthropic Guide, which teams up with global associations to address compassionate difficulties through imaginative arrangements. By utilizing the mastery of worldwide accomplices, Dubai plans to add to molding a future where information fills in as an impetus for positive change on a worldwide scale.

7.1 Investment in education and research as a key pillar of Dubai's growth.

Interest in Schooling and Exploration: The Foundation of Dubai's Development

In the bone-dry scenes of the Bedouin Bay, where the shining horizon of Dubai ascends against the desert skyline, a significant obligation to training and exploration has arisen as a critical mainstay of the city's development and change. The visionary administration of Dubai perceives that putting resources into information is an interest from here on out, laying the preparation for maintainable turn of events, advancement, and worldwide seriousness. This story unfurls against the setting of a city that has progressed from a provincial exchange center point to a worldwide focus of greatness, with instruction and examination filling in as the establishment for this exceptional excursion.

Instructive Advancement: From the Desert Sands to Scholarly Levels

Dubai's instructive scene has gone through a momentous development, reflecting the city's fast urbanization and financial enhancement.

Rewind to the early long stretches of Dubai, and one would find an unobtrusive school system essentially centered around meeting the fundamental requirements of a developing populace. Notwithstanding, as the city imagined a future past its exchanging roots, the seeds of instructive change were planted.

The foundation of the Dubai Information Town in 2003 denoted a crucial second in Dubai's instructive excursion. This free zone committed to instruction and preparing organizations laid the basis for the city's desires to turn into a center of information and learning. The initiative perceived the meaning of giving a helpful climate to instructive foundations to flourish, and this essential move prepared for a plenty of top notch colleges, universities, and preparing focuses to set up grounds in Dubai.

Today, Dubai stands pleased as the home to driving organizations like the Higher Schools of Innovation, Zayed College, and a large group of global colleges with branch grounds. The Dubai Global Scholastic City (DIAC), laid out in 2007, remains as a demonstration of the city's obligation to making a cooperative environment where scholarly greatness thrives. The scene of training in Dubai has moved from satisfying neighborhood needs to drawing in worldwide ability, making a blend of societies and thoughts inside the city's instructive organizations.

Interest in Human Resources: The Mohammed receptacle Rashid Al Maktoum Establishment

At the core of Dubai's instructive renaissance is the Mohammed receptacle Rashid Al Maktoum Establishment, a main impetus established in 2007 with a mission to enable people in the future through training. This establishment plays had a crucial impact in forming instructive strategies, giving grants, and supporting exploration drives that add to the general improvement of human resources in Dubai.

Grant programs started by the establishment have not just given open doors to Emirati understudies to seek after advanced education yet have likewise drawn in capable people from around the world to concentrate on in Dubai. By putting resources into human resources, Dubai isn't just tending to prompt monetary requirements but at the same time is sustaining a pool of talented experts who add to the city's drawn out development and intensity.

The establishment's multi-layered approach incorporates drives that range from giving admittance to quality schooling to supporting examination tries. This comprehensive methodology mirrors Dubai's comprehension that instruction isn't simply about granting information however is an impetus for individual and cultural turn of events.

Worldwide Coordinated efforts: Hoisting Instruction through Global Organizations

Dubai's obligation to instructive greatness is additionally highlighted by its hug of worldwide coordinated efforts.

Perceiving the worth of a worldwide point of view in schooling, the city has effectively looked for organizations with driving colleges and instructive establishments around the world. This cooperative methodology guarantees that understudies in Dubai are presented to assorted social encounters, showing approaches, and state of the art research.

The presence of worldwide grounds in Dubai has raised the nature of schooling as well as added to the city's worldwide allure. Understudies presently have the chance to acquire degrees from renowned organizations without leaving the dynamic and cosmopolitan climate of Dubai. This improves the instructive experience as well as cultivates a worldwide viewpoint among understudies, setting them up for a reality where lines are progressively obscured.

The Higher Schools of Innovation, for example, has produced organizations with foundations from nations like the US, Canada, and the Assembled Realm. These organizations bring an abundance of mastery and best practices to Dubai's instructive scene, guaranteeing that understudies get a top notch training that is lined up with worldwide guidelines.

Research Renaissance: Cultivating a Culture of Development

As Dubai tries to turn into a worldwide information center, its interest in research has become progressively urgent. The city perceives that genuine development is conceived out of a strong exploration environment that cultivates imagination, interest, and the quest for pivotal thoughts. Dubai's obligation to investigate isn't simply a mission for scholastic honors yet an essential move to situate itself at the bleeding edge of innovative headways, logical revelations, and answers for worldwide difficulties.

The Dubai Exploration and Development Culmination, a yearly assembling started by the Dubai Future Establishment, fills in as a stage for specialists, researchers, and pioneers to merge and share their experiences. This highest point not just features the city's obligation to sustaining a culture of development yet additionally gives a space to interdisciplinary coordinated efforts that can prompt extraordinary forward leaps.

The foundation of the Dubai Innovative work Place (DRDC) in 2016 addresses a huge achievement in Dubai's examination process. Zeroed in on key areas like medical care, energy, and man-made consciousness, the middle teams up with nearby and worldwide accomplices to drive advancement. By giving scientists cutting edge offices and monetary help, the DRDC catalyzes an exploration renaissance that adds to Dubai's development as a center point for state of the art arrangements.

Innovation Combination: Brilliant Learning for What's in store

Dubai's obligation to instructive development reaches out past conventional methodologies, embracing innovation as an incredible asset for change. The Shrewd Dubai Training drive, sent off in 2017, is a demonstration of the city's ground breaking way to deal with schooling.

This drive tries to use computerized innovations to improve the growth opportunity, planning understudies for a future where innovation is an essential piece of day to day existence.

The Mohammed receptacle Rashid Savvy Learning Project is a foundation of this computerized transformation in schooling. By giving understudies computerized gadgets, intelligent learning materials, and admittance to a tremendous vault of instructive assets, Dubai intends to establish a dynamic and intuitive learning climate. This upgrades the nature of schooling as well as furnishes understudies with computerized education abilities that are progressively fundamental in the advanced world.

Innovation coordination isn't restricted to the homeroom; it stretches out to the actual texture of Dubai's instructive establishments. The Dubai Future Institute, sent off by the Dubai Future Establishment, fills in as a stage for persistent mastering and expertise improvement. By offering projects, studios, and courses that influence arising advances, the foundation guarantees that people are furnished with the information and abilities expected to explore the intricacies representing things to come.

Business venture and Development: A Comprehensive Way to deal with Development

Dubai's interest in schooling and exploration goes past customary scholarly pursuits to envelop business venture and advancement. The city perceives that genuine development isn't exclusively determined by financial pointers however by an all encompassing methodology that sustains a culture of development. Drives like the Mohammed receptacle Rashid Development Asset offer monetary help to creative ventures and new companies, cultivating a feeling of business that adds to Dubai's financial enhancement.

Free zones devoted to explicit businesses, for example, Dubai Web City and Dubai Information Park, make biological systems where new companies, innovation organizations, and research establishments can team up. These zones draw in worldwide ability as well as work with the trading of thoughts and the advancement of creative arrangements. Dubai's obligation to sustaining a culture of development is an essential move that positions the city as a worldwide center point where thoughts are changed into unmistakable arrangements.

7.2 The establishment of world-class educational institutions.

The Foundation of Elite Instructive Organizations: Dubai's Scholarly Renaissance

Settled between the brilliant hills of the Bedouin Desert and the turquoise waters of the Middle Eastern Bay, Dubai has gone through a terrific change from an unassuming exchanging port to a worldwide center of business, culture, and development. At the core of this transformation lies the foundation of top notch instructive establishments, an essential move that has raised Dubai's status on the worldwide stage. This story unfurls against the background of a city that, with visionary premonition, perceived the groundbreaking force of training in molding its fate.

The Early Years: An Unassuming Start

Dubai's excursion towards turning into a reference point of instruction started with humble starting points. In the early many years of the twentieth hundred years, the city's instructive scene was set apart by a shortage of formal organizations. Conventional Quranic schools, known as "kuttab," assumed an essential part in giving fundamental training to the young. Nonetheless, as Dubai set out on a direction of modernization, it became obvious that a more strong instructive foundation was fundamental for the city's supported development.

Dubai Information Town: A Change in perspective

The defining moment in Dubai's instructive direction came in 2003 with the foundation of the Dubai Information Town. This aggressive task denoted a change in outlook, flagging the city's obligation to encouraging an information based economy. As a free zone devoted to instructive foundations and preparing focuses, Information Town gave a sustaining climate to scholastic greatness, research tries, and abilities improvement. It established the groundwork for the deluge of top notch colleges and universities that would before long call Dubai home.

Higher Schools of Innovation (HCT): Spearheading Advanced education

Among the pioneers in Dubai's instructive scene is the Higher Schools of Innovation (HCT). Laid out in 1988, HCT assumed a urgent part in offering advanced education in applied sciences and innovation, taking special care of the developing necessities of the gig market. HCT's obligation to furnishing quality instruction lined up with global principles situated Dubai as an objective for higher learning.

Throughout the long term, HCT has developed to turn into the biggest advanced education organization in the UAE, with numerous grounds across Dubai and different emirates. Its accentuation on commonsense, involved learning has engaged understudies with the abilities important to contribute genuinely to Dubai's blossoming economy.

Zayed College: Sustaining Future Pioneers

Zayed College, named after the visionary principal architect of the UAE, Sheik Zayed canister Ruler Al Nahyan, was laid out in 1998. This organization, with grounds in both Abu Dhabi and Dubai, assumes a urgent part in engaging Emirati ladies and men with information and abilities. Zayed College's obligation to scholarly greatness, examination, and local area commitment has contributed essentially to Dubai's rise as an instructive force to be reckoned with.

The grounds in Dubai, arranged in the core of the city, mirrors the obligation to giving understudies an energetic and comprehensive learning climate. The accentuation on orientation equity and engaging the young highlights Dubai's devotion to cultivating a general public where training is an impetus for positive cultural change.

Dubai Global Scholastic City (DIAC): A Cooperative Biological system

The Dubai Global Scholastic City (DIAC), laid out in 2007, arose as a demonstration of Dubai's obligation to making a cooperative biological system for scholarly organizations. DIAC fills in as a center where colleges, research focuses, and scholastic foundations from around the world exist together. This cooperative climate cultivates interdisciplinary coordinated efforts, information trade, and a unique collaboration that impels training higher than ever.

With north of 25 worldwide colleges offering a different scope of projects, DIAC has changed Dubai into worldwide schooling objective. Understudies have the chance to sign up for programs going from business and designing to expressions and sciences, guaranteeing an extensive and balanced instructive experience.

Worldwide Associations: Raising Scholastic Principles

Dubai's rising in the domain of schooling is additionally highlighted by its proactive quest for worldwide associations with prestigious global organizations. The city's initiative perceived right off the bat that joint efforts with regarded colleges wouldn't just upgrade the nature of training yet in addition add to Dubai's standing as a worldwide schooling center point.

The presentation of worldwide grounds in Dubai has brought a different scope of scholarly points of view and techniques to the city. Remarkable colleges, including the College of Wollongong, Heriot-Watt College, and Middlesex College, have laid out a presence in Dubai, furnishing understudies with the chance to procure degrees from foundations with a worldwide standing for scholastic greatness.

These worldwide organizations draw in global understudies to Dubai as well as make a mixture of societies inside the city's instructive establishments. The trading of thoughts and encounters improves the scholarly climate, planning understudies to explore the intricacies of a globalized world.

Key Preparation and Vision: The Mohammed receptacle Rashid Al Maktoum Establishment

At the core of Dubai's instructive renaissance is the Mohammed canister Rashid Al Maktoum Establishment. Established in 2007, the establishment bears the name of Dubai's visionary chief, Sheik Mohammed receptacle Rashid Al Maktoum. With a mission to enable people in the future through training, the establishment plays had a critical impact in forming instructive strategies, giving grants, and supporting exploration drives.

The establishment's diverse methodology envelops grants for Emirati understudies, research awards for scholastics, and drives pointed toward encouraging advancement in training. By putting resources into human resources and advancing a culture of deep rooted learning, the establishment guarantees that instruction turns into a main impetus behind Dubai's supported development and improvement.

Dubai's Different Instructive Scene: A Worldwide Blend

The foundation of elite instructive establishments in Dubai has changed the city into a worldwide mixture of societies, thoughts, and goals. With a different scope of projects, from designing and business to artistic expression and humanities, Dubai's instructive scene mirrors the city's obligation to offering a complete and comprehensive growth opportunity.

The worldwide understudy local area in Dubai has prospered, attracted to the city's dynamic mix of scholarly greatness, social variety, and unrivaled foundation. This inundation of worldwide ability not just adds to the social energy of Dubai yet additionally positions the city as a center for culturally diverse exchange and cooperation.

7.3 The role of research and innovation in shaping the city's future.

The Job of Exploration and Development in Molding Dubai's Future: A Mechanical Embroidery

In the core of the Bedouin Bay, in the midst of the glimmering towers and clamoring roads of Dubai, a quiet upheaval is in progress — one driven by the persevering quest for examination and development. The city, when characterized by its exchanging legacy and sandy scenes, has decisively situated itself as a worldwide center for state of the art innovations and earth shattering revelations. This story unfurls against the setting of a cityscape that has developed from a provincial exchange place to an image of cutting edge urbanism, moved by a pledge to research and advancement.

Dubai's Visionary Jump into Advancement

Dubai's excursion into the domain of examination and advancement is meaningful of its initiative's visionary way to deal with city-building. The Dubai Future Establishment, laid out in 2016, fills in as an impetus for this extraordinary excursion. With an order to situate Dubai at the cutting edge of worldwide advancement, the establishment plays had a significant impact in molding the city's plan for examination, improvement, and mechanical progression.

The send off of the Dubai Future Plan, an exhaustive guide framing key drives for the city's future, highlights Dubai's obligation to saddling the force of development. This plan includes areas going from medical care and schooling to transportation and manageability, flagging an all encompassing way to deal with forming Dubai's predetermination through research-driven arrangements.

The Dubai Innovative work Place (DRDC): A Center for Development

At the core of Dubai's examination tries is the Dubai Innovative work Place (DRDC), laid out in 2016. Zeroed in on key areas like medical care, energy, and man-made brainpower, the middle fills in as a core for cooperative examination endeavors.

By uniting nearby and worldwide specialists, the DRDC expects to drive development, address squeezing difficulties, and add to Dubai's rise as a worldwide information center.

The DRDC's drives length a range of examination exercises, from basic logical requests to applied research projects with direct ramifications for industry and society. By giving cutting edge research framework and monetary help, the middle establishes a climate helpful for historic revelations. This obligation to explore greatness positions Dubai as an objective where the limits of information are constantly pushed, and where answers for worldwide difficulties are effectively looked for.

Yearly Dubai Exploration and Development Culmination: A Worldwide Juncture of Brains

The yearly Dubai Exploration and Development Culmination, started by the Dubai Future Establishment, fills in as a demonstration of the city's obligation to cultivating a culture of development. This highest point unites specialists, researchers, and pioneers from around the world, giving a stage to feature leap forwards, examine arising patterns, and diagram the course for the eventual fate of exploration in Dubai.

The culmination is something other than a get-together of brains; it is a festival of Dubai's desire to be at the front of worldwide exploration tries. By cultivating coordinated efforts and interdisciplinary trades, the highest point adds to the city's situation as a center where various viewpoints meet to address complex difficulties. It supports that development is definitely not a single pursuit yet a cooperative exertion that rises above geological limits.

Gallery Representing things to come: A Living Research facility of Development

Planned to open its entryways in 2023, the Gallery Representing things to come remains as an actual sign of Dubai's obligation to being a living lab of development. This famous design is imagined as a historical center as well as a powerful space where researchers, scientists, and creatives meet up to investigate arising innovations, try different things with groundbreaking thoughts, and add to molding what's to come.

The Exhibition hall Representing things to come goes past the customary idea of a gallery; it is intended to be a hatchery of thoughts, a proving ground for models, and a feature of developments that can possibly change social orders. As a demonstration of Dubai's desire, the gallery represents a guarantee to making development open, connecting with, and fundamental to the texture of daily existence.

Innovation Combination: Savvy Dubai Drives

Dubai's obligation to development reaches out past exploration organizations and highest points; it pervades the actual texture of the city through drives like Brilliant Dubai. Sent off in 2013, the Shrewd Dubai drive means to change the city into a brilliant, consistent, and productive metropolitan climate.

By coordinating state of the art advances, information investigation, and computerized reasoning, Savvy Dubai imagines a city where development upgrades the personal satisfaction for occupants and guests the same.

One of the vital mainstays of Brilliant Dubai is the execution of blockchain innovation, determined to turn into the world's first blockchain-fueled government by 2020. This creative way to deal with administration improves straightforwardness and security as well as positions Dubai as a worldwide innovator in utilizing blockchain for public administrations.

Additionally, the Dubai Information Drive supports Brilliant Dubai's endeavors to tackle the force of information for better direction. By amassing and breaking down information from different sources, the city intends to acquire bits of knowledge that can illuminate approaches, streamline administrations, and improve by and large metropolitan preparation.

Development Regions: Center points of Innovative Headway

Dubai's obligation to development is additionally exemplified by the foundation of devoted advancement locale inside the city. Regions like Dubai Web City, Dubai Silicon Desert spring, and Dubai Science Park act as centers where innovation organizations, new businesses, and research establishments mix to drive headways in different fields.

Dubai Web City, laid out in 2000, is a free monetary zone that has an energetic biological system of innovation organizations. From global partnerships to arising new companies, this area cultivates a climate where thoughts prosper, and joint effort is empowered. It has turned into a magnet for worldwide tech goliaths hoping to lay out a presence in the locale.

Dubai Silicon Desert garden, established in 2004, centers around cultivating development in the field of microelectronics and semiconductors. The locale gives a stage to organizations participated in innovative work, situating Dubai as a center point for mechanical progressions in the gadgets business.

Dubai Science Park, introduced in 2005, is committed to the existence sciences, energy, and ecological areas. By giving cutting edge foundation and a cooperative climate, the recreation area catalyzes exploration and development in basic regions that line up with Dubai's essential objectives for supportability and medical care.

Worldwide Coordinated efforts: Dubai Future Gas pedals

Dubai's obligation to advancement isn't restricted to neighborhood tries; it effectively looks for worldwide joint efforts to drive progress. The Dubai Future Gas pedals program, sent off by the Dubai Future Establishment, represents this methodology. The program unites government elements and inventive organizations from around the world to co-make answers for difficulties looked by the public area.

Through associations with worldwide pioneers, Dubai tries to use outer aptitude and state of the art advancements to address cultural difficulties. This cooperative model guarantees that the arrangements created are imaginative as well as have genuine applications. The Dubai Future Gas pedals program positions Dubai as a testbed for groundbreaking arrangements that can have a worldwide effect.

Maintainability and Green Development: A Comprehensive Methodology

Dubai's obligation to development stretches out to supportability, with an emphasis on green drives that add to the city's natural objectives. The Dubai Clean Energy Methodology 2050, sent off in 2015, frames a guide for differentiating the city's energy blend and expanding the portion of clean energy.

The Mohammed canister Rashid Al Maktoum Sun powered Park, perhaps of the biggest sun based park on the planet, is a demonstration of Dubai's obligation to sustainable power. The recreation area expects to create 5,000 megawatts of clean energy by 2030, fundamentally diminishing the city's carbon impression.

Notwithstanding enormous scope projects, Dubai effectively advances green development through drives like the Green Asset. This asset upholds innovative work projects that add to natural manageability, lining up with the city's vision of turning into a worldwide forerunner in green advances.

Chapter 8

"People of Dubai: A Tapestry of Cultures"

Individuals of Dubai: An Embroidery of Societies

In the core of the Bedouin Landmass, where the brilliant ridges meet the sky blue waters of the Middle Eastern Bay, Dubai remains as a worldwide city that entices with its stunning horizon and social energy. Past the structural wonders and financial ability lies the genuine pith of Dubai — individuals who call this city home. An embroidery woven from strings of different societies, individuals of Dubai all in all add to the city's special personality, making an agreeable mix of custom and innovation.

Social Blend: Supporting Variety

Dubai's change from a humble exchanging station to a cosmopolitan center is reflected in its segment scene. Individuals of Dubai address a rich embroidery of societies, nationalities, and foundations, making a blend that recognizes the city on the worldwide stage. Embracing variety has been a foundation of Dubai's prosperity, cultivating a climate where people from around the world can coincide, team up, and add to the city's dynamic development.

The UAE's key geological area at the intersection of Asia, Europe, and Africa has generally made it a mixture of societies and exchange. Dubai, with its entryway strategy and obligation to resilience, has embraced this variety, drawing in ostracizes looking for open doors and a greater of life. Today, the city's populace contains a greater part of ostracizes, with Emiratis shaping a lively center that invests heavily in protecting the social legacy of the locale.

The Emirati Personality: Connecting Custom and Advancement

At the core of Dubai's social embroidered artwork are the Emiratis, the local individuals of the Unified Bedouin Emirates. Emirati personality is well established in the rich customs of the Bedouin Promontory, with a legacy that traverses hundreds of years of traveling life, pearl plunging, and exchange. Notwithstanding the quick modernization and metropolitan turn of events, Emiratis invest wholeheartedly in saving their social legacy, obvious in the proceeded with festivity of conventional celebrations, like the yearly Al Marmoom Legacy Celebration, where camel hustling, falconry, and customary music become the dominant focal point.

The initiative's obligation to saving Emirati culture is exemplified by drives like the Al Shindagha Exhibition hall, which offers a brief look into the city's set of experiences, customs, and the excursion from a fishing town to a worldwide city. The conservation of the Arabic language, customary dress, and social practices mirrors Dubai's devotion to keeping serious areas of strength for a character in the midst of the cosmopolitan clamor.

Exile People group: A Worldwide Mosaic

Dubai's ascent as a worldwide city is intrinsically attached to the convergence of exiles who have brought their abilities, gifts, and social variety to the city. Exiles from more than 200 identities structure a lively mosaic, making a one of a kind social embroidery that recognizes Dubai as a really global objective. Whether it's the clamoring markets of Deira, the multicultural neighborhoods of Al Barsha, or the upscale locale of Downtown Dubai, each side of the city mirrors the different foundations and accounts of its occupants.

Networks from South Asia, the Center East, Europe, Africa, and the Americas coincide, adding to the city's multicultural climate. From clamoring souks where brokers deal in horde dialects to worldwide schools that take special care of a worldwide understudy body, Dubai's day to day routine is a demonstration of the amicable concurrence of various societies. Exiles see as a usual hangout spot in Dubai, where social variety isn't simply endured however celebrated.

Social Festivals: A Schedule of Variety

Dubai's obligation to encouraging social variety is apparent in its schedule of festivities, which traverses strict, public, and worldwide celebrations. From the brilliant showcases of firecrackers during New Year's Eve to the gravity of Ramadan, Dubai's occupants meet up to commend, offer, and regard each other's customs.

The yearly Dubai Shopping Celebration is a perfect representation of the city's commitment to inclusivity. During this extended party, guests and inhabitants the same are blessed to receive a worldwide shopping and diversion exhibition. Customary souks, close by global brands, offer a different shopping experience that takes special care of the shifted preferences of Dubai's multicultural populace.

Strict Resistance: Spots of Love for All Beliefs

Dubai's obligation to strict resistance is appeared in the different cluster of spots of love that dab the cityscape. While the UAE is an Islamic express, the constitution ensures opportunity of religion, and Dubai fills in as a model for conjunction.

The Stupendous Mosque, with its staggering engineering and ability to have large number of admirers, remains as an image of Islamic confidence. Notwithstanding, Dubai is likewise home to chapels, sanctuaries, and temples, taking care of the profound necessities of the different exile networks. The St. Mary's Catholic Church, the Gurudwara Master Nanak Darbar, and the Hindu sanctuary Shiva and Krishna

Mandir are only a couple of instances of the city's obligation to giving spaces to different strict practices.

Social Areas: Supporting Artistic expression

Dubai's obligation to social variety stretches out to human expression, with devoted locale and occasions that feature the worldwide embroidered artwork of imaginative articulation. Alserkal Road in Al Quoz, for example, is a flourishing expressions center that unites contemporary workmanship exhibitions, studios, and theaters. It fills in as a stage for neighborhood and global specialists to exhibit their work, encouraging multifaceted discourse through the general language of craftsmanship.

Furthermore, the Dubai Show, an engineering wonder in Midtown Dubai, has exhibitions that range the social range — from Western old style music to customary Arabic exhibitions. The Dubai Global Film Celebration, albeit briefly on hold, has been a stage for producers from around the world to grandstand their work, adding one more layer to the city's social texture.

Culinary Variety: A Gala for the Faculties

Dubai's culinary scene is an impression of its different populace, offering a gastronomic excursion that traverses mainlands. From customary Emirati dishes like Al Harees to global cooking styles that reach from Indian and Pakistani to Italian and Japanese, Dubai's feasting choices are essentially as changed as its occupants. Neighborhoods like Al Fahidi and Al Satwa are known for their different scope of diners, giving a culinary mixture that takes care of each and every taste bud.

The yearly Dubai Food Celebration is a demonstration of the city's obligation to culinary variety. The celebration unites nearby and worldwide cooks, offering a gala for the faculties that features the worldwide flavors that characterize Dubai's culinary scene.

Local area Drives: Associating Lives

Past the fabulousness and excitement, Dubai's feeling of local area is sustained through different drives that advance inclusivity and social attachment. The "Dubai Cares" crusade, for example, centers around giving training to oppressed kids worldwide, encapsulating the soul of giving that is profoundly imbued in the city's ethos.

Local area occasions like the "Stroll for Training" unite individuals from varying backgrounds, underscoring the common obligation of adding to a superior world. Such drives exhibit Dubai's obligation to supporting its own local area as well as expanding some assistance universally.

8.1 The multicultural fabric of Dubai's society.

The Multicultural Texture of Dubai's General public: An Embroidery of Solidarity

In the core of the Bedouin Desert, where brilliant sands meet the shining waters of the Middle Eastern Bay, lies Dubai — a city that rises above its geological limits to arise as a worldwide mixture of societies. Past its famous horizon and stunning framework, Dubai's actual abundance lies in individuals — the different networks have met up to wind around a dynamic embroidery of solidarity. This multicultural texture, unpredictably strung with the practices, dialects, and customs of the world, recognizes Dubai as a city where variety isn't simply embraced however celebrated.

Worldwide Assembly: Ostracizes in Dubai

Dubai's multiculturalism tracks down its foundations in the worldwide assembly of exiles from each edge of the globe. Drawn by the commitment of monetary open doors, an exclusive requirement of living, and a cosmopolitan climate, exiles make up a critical larger part of Dubai's populace. The city's charming mix of innovation and custom fills in as an attractive power, drawing in people with different abilities, gifts, and goals.

Strolling through the neighborhoods of Dubai uncovers a microcosm of the world's societies. From the fragrant flavors of the Indian business sectors in Deira to the enthusiastic babble in Filipino local meetings, Dubai exemplifies a worldwide town where various societies coincide amicably. Ostracizes have not just turned into an indispensable piece of Dubai's labor force however have likewise added to the city's social wealth, making a novel personality that rises above public limits.

Emirati Neighborliness: Saving Custom In the midst of Variety

At the center of Dubai's multicultural texture is the local Emirati populace, whose unfaltering cordiality has been a sign of the city's personality. Emiratis assume a vital part in safeguarding the social legacy of the district, guaranteeing that conventional practices and values stay fundamental to the city's story.

In the clamoring souks of Dubai, where dealers from assorted foundations participate in enlivened discussions, Emirati vendors gladly feature their legacy. The glow with which Emiratis invite guests into their homes during events like Ramadan encourages a feeling of local area and extensions social holes. Conventional occasions like weddings, where Emirati customs are unpredictably woven into the festival, offer a brief look into the rich embroidery of Emirati life in the midst of the multicultural scene.

Social Articulations: Celebrations and Festivities

Dubai's schedule is interspersed with a different exhibit of celebrations and festivities that mirror the multicultural embroidery of its general public. During Diwali, the Hindu celebration of lights, the night sky over Dubai is enlightened with brilliant presentations, resounding with the glad festivals of the Indian people group. Essentially, the dynamic celebrations of Eid al-Fitr, denoting the finish of Ramadan, join individuals from different social foundations out of a sense of common concordance.

The yearly Worldwide Town, a social event that unites structures addressing various nations, exhibits the variety of Dubai's populace. From African drumbeats to Asian dance exhibitions, the occasion is a demonstration of the city's obligation to giving a stage to social trade and understanding. Through these festivals, Dubai not just recognizes the different starting points of its occupants however effectively empowers the sharing of customs, cultivating a feeling of having a place among its multicultural occupants.

Instructive Mosaic: Sustaining Worldwide Points of view

Dubai's obligation to training mirrors how its might interpret the vital job schools and colleges play in molding a worldwide outlook. Global schools in Dubai take special care of understudies from a large number of ethnicities, giving a climate where social trade isn't just supported yet implanted in the educational plan. Understudies grow up close by peers from different foundations, encouraging a feeling of transparency, resistance, and regard for various societies.

Colleges in Dubai, in a joint effort with worldwide foundations, further add to the city's multicultural ethos. These foundations act as center points where understudies from around the world meet up to seek after advanced education. The trading of thoughts, points of view, and encounters in such instructive settings adds one more layer to the social texture of Dubai, setting up the cutting edge for a globalized world.

Language Embroidery: An Ensemble of Voices

Dubai's semantic scene is an ensemble of voices, repeating the large number of dialects spoken by its occupants. While Arabic fills in as the authority language, English has arisen as a most widely used language, working with correspondence among individuals from different semantic foundations. Moreover, the city reverberates with the hints of Tagalog, Urdu, Hindi, Bengali, and incalculable different dialects, making an amicable etymological mosaic that reflects the city's multicultural soul.

The variety of dialects isn't simply a pragmatic need yet an impression of Dubai's obligation to inclusivity. Multilingual signage, government records, and client support communications take special care of the semantic variety of the populace, guaranteeing that everybody feels invited and comprehended. This etymological embroidery adds to the cosmopolitan environment of Dubai, where correspondence is a scaffold that interfaces instead of partitions.

Culinary Combination: A Worldwide Banquet for the Sense of taste

One of the most substantial articulations of Dubai's multiculturalism is tracked down in its culinary scene. The city's eating scene is a worldwide banquet, offering a different cluster of foods that mirrors the changed preferences and inclinations of its occupants. From road side shawarma slows down to Michelin-featured eateries, Dubai's culinary contributions length the globe, taking special care of the palates of people from various social foundations.

Neighborhoods like Al Rigga and Al Karama are known for their culinary variety, with eateries serving dishes from Lebanon, Pakistan, the Philippines, and then some. Food celebrations, like the Dubai Food Celebration and Taste of Dubai, praise the city's gastronomic extravagance, welcoming inhabitants and guests to leave on a culinary excursion all over the planet. Dubai's food culture is a demonstration of its open hug of different culinary practices, making a tangible encounter that reflects the multicultural energy of the city.

Sports and Entertainment: A Bringing together Field

In the realm of sports, Dubai fills in as a binding together field where people from different social foundations meet up to commend physicality and rivalry. Global games, like the Dubai Tennis Titles, the Dubai Rugby Sevens, and the Dubai World Cup, draw in members and observers from around the world.

The city's obligation to sports stretches out past expert contests to grassroots drives that empower support at the local area level. Global groups and associations in different games give stages to people to participate in amicable rivalry, cultivating fellowship among individuals with various identities and foundations.

Local area Drives: Connecting Partitions

Dubai's obligation to multiculturalism isn't bound to day to day cooperations but at the same time is reflected in different local area drives that effectively try to connect partitions. Associations and grassroots developments, for example, the Local area Improvement Authority's (CDA) "Together We Are Great" crusade sent off during the Coronavirus pandemic, highlight the city's devotion to encouraging a feeling of fortitude among its occupants.

The "Dubai Cares" crusade, zeroed in on giving schooling to oppressed youngsters universally, addresses one more feature of Dubai's obligation to rewarding networks past its lines. These drives feature the interconnectedness of Dubai's inhabitants and their common obligation regarding the prosperity of the worldwide local area.

8.2 Stories of expatriates and locals contributing to the city's diversity.

Accounts of Ostracizes and Local people: Sustaining Dubai's Variety

Dubai, with its shining high rises and cosmopolitan feeling, isn't simply a city of cement and glass; it is a residing demonstration of the tales of people who have decided to call it home. Exiles from around the world and local people the same contribute their extraordinary accounts to the dynamic embroidery that characterizes Dubai's variety. These accounts wind around together to frame a story of solidarity, flexibility, and shared desires that rise above social limits.

A Worldwide Mixture: The Ostracize Insight

For some exiles, Dubai addresses a chance for proficient development, self-awareness, and openness to a multicultural climate. Take the tale of Maria, a promoting proficient from the Philippines, who moved to Dubai looking for new difficulties. At first drawn by the city's dynamic work market, Maria before long found that Dubai offered something beyond profession open doors; it gave a space where various societies could coincide amicably.

Maria's experience reflects that of endless ostracizes who have discovered a feeling of having a place in Dubai. Past the difficulties of adjusting to another climate, ostracizes frequently find a steady local area that rises above public lines. The fellowship framed in working environments, neighborhoods, and groups of friends turns into a wellspring of solidarity, changing the ostracize insight into a common excursion of development and social trade.

Building Scaffolds: Local people Embracing Worldwide Viewpoints

While ostracizes carry an abundance of variety to Dubai, the tales of local people embracing worldwide viewpoints are similarly convincing. Ahmed, a youthful Emirati business visionary, is a brilliant illustration of the changing elements inside the neighborhood local area. Propelled by his encounters concentrating abroad, Ahmed got back to Dubai with a dream to coordinate worldwide prescribed procedures into his privately-run company's.

Ahmed's story mirrors a more extensive pattern among Emirati youth who are progressively looking for worldwide openness and embracing different points of view. The longing to mix custom with development has prompted a social renaissance inside the neighborhood local area, where youthful Emiratis are at the very front of drives that overcome any barrier among custom and innovation.

Creative Joint efforts: The Matter of Variety

The business scene in Dubai is a phase where various stories unfurl, driven by the cooperative endeavors of ostracizes and local people the same. Consider the narrative of Sarah and Omar, a multicultural couple who established a tech startup in Dubai. Sarah, initially from the US, and Omar, an Emirati, consolidated their abilities and social foundations to make an organization that flourished with variety.

Their process is symbolic of Dubai's pioneering soul, where people from various regions of the planet meet up to develop and make. The city's business biological system gives a prolific ground to such joint efforts, encouraging a climate where different viewpoints are invited as well as fundamental for progress.

Social Extensions: Exiles Embracing Emirati Customs

One of the interesting parts of Dubai's variety is the readiness of ostracizes to embrace and celebrate nearby practices. Stories flourish of ostracizes effectively taking part in Emirati comprehensive developments, from conventional weddings to camel dashing celebrations. The receptiveness to finding out about and regarding nearby traditions makes a feeling of common comprehension and appreciation.

The narrative of Julia, an European exile, hangs out in this specific situation. Captivated by the extravagance of Emirati culture, Julia willingly volunteered to learn Arabic and drench herself in nearby practices. Her veritable premium not just gained her the appreciation of her Emirati partners yet additionally filled in to act as an illustration of how people from various foundations can fabricate spans through social trade.

Instructive Intersection: Ostracizes Forming What's in store

Training is a urgent field where ostracizes and local people merge, forming the fate of Dubai's multicultural society. The city's global schools are center points of variety, where educators and understudies from different foundations meet up in a common quest for information. The accounts of instructors like Dr. Singh, an Indian exile who has been showing in Dubai for more than 10 years, outline the groundbreaking job of training in cultivating understanding and resistance.

Dr. Singh's enthusiasm for educating goes past the educational program; he effectively urges understudies to investigate and value the different societies addressed in their study halls. His story mirrors the bigger account of teachers assuming a significant part in sustaining the up and coming age of worldwide residents who esteem variety as a strength as opposed to a distinction.

Clinical Wonders: Medical services Experts Joining for a Typical Reason

The medical care area in Dubai is a microcosm of worldwide cooperation, with exile and nearby medical services experts working next to each other to guarantee the prosperity of the local area. The account of Dr. Patel, a specialist from India, and Dr. Al Mansoori, an Emirati doctor, represents the cooperative soul inside Dubai's clinical local area.

Dr. Patel, attracted to Dubai by the cutting edge clinical offices and potential open doors for proficient development, found a strong climate that empowered information trade. Dr. Al Mansoori, thusly, appreciated the variety of aptitude brought by his global partners. Together, they dealt with notable clinical examination projects that exhibited the collaboration among neighborhood and worldwide points of view in propelling medical services.

Local area Drives: Exiles and Local people Holding Hands

Dubai's obligation to local area improvement is reflected in drives that unite ostracizes and local people for a typical reason. The tale of the "Embrace an Ocean side" crusade, where occupants, regardless of their ethnicity, tell the truth and safeguard the sea shores of Dubai, highlights the common obligation towards the city's current circumstance.

These people group driven drives add to Dubai's maintainability objectives as well as act as stages for ostracizes and local people to team up beyond proficient settings. From ecological preservation undertakings to beneficent undertakings, these accounts of aggregate activity feature the interconnectedness of Dubai's occupants in having a beneficial outcome on their local area.

Widespread developments: Celebrations Joining Hearts

Dubai's lively schedule of comprehensive developments and celebrations gives a phase where ostracizes and local people feature their gifts and customs. The yearly Sikka Workmanship Fair, for example, unites craftsmen from different foundations, encouraging an imaginative trade that rises above social limits. Also, the Emirates Carrier Celebration of Writing commends the composed word, drawing in writers, artists, and writing aficionados from around the world.

These comprehensive developments not just grandstand the variety of ability inside Dubai yet in addition make spaces where ostracizes and local people can take part in significant discussions about workmanship, writing, and shared human encounters. The narratives that rise out of these occasions are a demonstration of the city's obligation to supporting a social scene that mirrors the wealth of its multicultural society.

Comprehensive Spaces: Exiles Adding to Social Congruity

Dubai's public spaces, whether parks, shopping centers, or social locale, are fields where exiles effectively add to the city's social concordance.

The narrative of the "Understanding Country" crusade, started by a gathering of ostracize teachers, represents the force of inclusivity in making positive change. The mission planned to give books to kids out of luck, rising above social and semantic boundaries to advance the all inclusive worth of instruction.

Ostracizes, through their commitment to such drives, assume a pivotal part in encouraging a feeling of social obligation and local area administration. These accounts highlight the possibility that Dubai's public spaces are actual scenes as well as shared conditions where different people meet up for everyone's benefit.

8.3 Social initiatives and community programs that foster harmony.

Social Drives and Local area Projects: Encouraging Agreement in Dubai

Dubai, with its transcending high rises and clamoring roads, isn't simply a city of financial ability yet an energetic local area where social drives and local area programs assume a critical part together as one among its different inhabitants. Past the marvelousness and fabulousness, these drives act as strings that wind around together the texture of Dubai's multicultural society, making a feeling of solidarity and shared liability. From natural supportability to social protection, these projects add to the city's ethos of inclusivity and social congruity.

Practical City Drives: Sustaining a Green Dubai

Dubai's obligation to supportability is obvious in a heap of drives pointed toward making an all the more ecologically cognizant and green city. The narrative of the Maintainable City, a spearheading private turn of events, fills in as a model of Dubai's devotion to offsetting urbanization with biological obligation. With highlights like sun powered chargers, reusing offices, and metropolitan cultivating, the Economical City gives a feasible living climate as well as fills in as an instructive center for occupants and guests the same.

Local area gardens inside neighborhoods, tree-establishing drives, and reusing efforts are a portion of the drives that effectively draw in occupants in reasonable practices. These projects add to Dubai's natural objectives as well as make a feeling of local area possession and obligation towards the city's environmental prosperity.

Embrace an Ocean side: Joining Occupants for Beach front Protection

Dubai's shocking shore isn't simply a position of diversion yet in addition a point of convergence for local area commitment in natural protection. The "Embrace an Ocean side" crusade, where inhabitants from different foundations tell the truth and safeguard Dubai's sea shores, epitomizes the force of local area driven drives. Coordinated by ecological associations, volunteers, including exiles and local people, assemble consistently to eliminate trash and bring issues to light about the significance of seaside preservation.

This program rises above social and public limits, joining occupants under a typical reason — safeguarding the regular excellence of Dubai's shores. Past the prompt ecological effect, Take on an Ocean side encourages a feeling of shared liability and local area pride.

Understanding Country: Exiles and Local people Advancing Instruction

Instruction is a foundation of Dubai's vision for a prosperous and agreeable society. The "Understanding Country" crusade, started by the UAE's VP and State leader, Sheik Mohammed receptacle Rashid Al Maktoum, is a demonstration of the city's obligation to advancing proficiency and training. Ostracizes and local people the same add to this mission, which expects to give books to kids deprived across the globe.

From teachers to understudies, people from different social foundations effectively take part in book drives, pledge drives, and understanding occasions. This drive advances the all inclusive worth of training as well as makes a feeling of fortitude among Dubai's inhabitants, rising above social and etymological contrasts.

Local area Improvement Authority (CDA): Spanning Holes and Engaging People group

The People group Improvement Authority (CDA) in Dubai fills in as a central member in carrying out friendly drives that address the different requirements of the city's occupants. Through different projects, the CDA centers around cultivating social union, supporting weak populaces, and enabling networks.

One striking drive is the "Together We Are Great" crusade sent off during the Coronavirus pandemic. This mission saw coordinated effort between government elements, organizations, and people, the two ostracizes and local people, to offer fundamental help to those impacted by the pandemic. From circulating dinners to supporting cutting edge laborers, the drive displayed the strength of Dubai's people group in the midst of emergency.

Dubai Cares: A Worldwide Way to deal with Training

Dubai's obligation to instruction stretches out past its boundaries through drives like Dubai Cares. This generous association, drove by Sheik Mohammed receptacle Rashid Al Maktoum, plans to internationally work on youngsters' admittance to quality instruction. Ostracizes and local people effectively add to Dubai Cares through gathering pledges occasions, volunteerism, and mindfulness crusades.

The association's undertakings range from building schools and giving instructive assets to executing programs that address worldwide training difficulties. Dubai Cares mirrors Dubai's worldwide viewpoint as well as highlights the city's devotion to being a positive power in resolving cultural issues on a worldwide scale.

Comprehensive Spaces: Dubai Configuration Region (d3)

Dubai Configuration Region (d3) is a center for the innovative local area, where specialists, originators, and business visionaries from different foundations meet to feature their gifts. This comprehensive space effectively advances social trade and joint effort. The yearly Sikka Workmanship Fair, facilitated in d3, is a festival of the UAE's imaginative local area, drawing in members from different identities and cultivating a feeling of shared imagination.

d3 fills in as a model for comprehensive metropolitan preparation, giving a stage to social articulation and discourse. The locale's drives, like craftsmanship establishments, plan displays, and local area occasions, make a lively climate that supports inhabitants, exiles, and sightseers to draw in with the city's social scene.

Dubai Cares: A Worldwide Way to deal with Instruction

Dubai's obligation to schooling stretches out past its boundaries through drives like Dubai Cares. This generous association, drove by Sheik Mohammed container Rashid Al Maktoum, intends to worldwide work on youngsters' admittance to quality schooling. Exiles and local people effectively add to Dubai Cares through raising support occasions, volunteerism, and mindfulness crusades.

The association's tasks range from building schools and giving instructive assets to carrying out programs that address worldwide training difficulties. Dubai Cares mirrors Dubai's worldwide point of view as well as highlights the city's devotion to being a positive power in resolving cultural issues on a worldwide scale.

Comprehensive Spaces: Dubai Configuration Region (d3)

Dubai Configuration Region (d3) is a center point for the innovative local area, where craftsmen, fashioners, and business people from different foundations unite to grandstand their gifts. This comprehensive space effectively advances social trade and cooperation. The yearly Sikka Workmanship Fair, facilitated in d3, is a festival of the UAE's imaginative local area, drawing in members from different identities and encouraging a feeling of shared inventiveness.

d3 fills in as a model for comprehensive metropolitan preparation, giving a stage to social articulation and discourse. The locale's drives, like workmanship establishments, plan displays, and local area occasions, make an energetic environment that empowers inhabitants, exiles, and travelers to draw in with the city's social scene.

Dubai Chemical imbalance Community: A Model for Comprehensive Consideration

The Dubai Chemical imbalance Community is a spearheading foundation that epitomizes Dubai's obligation to giving comprehensive consideration to people with chemical imbalance. Ostracizes and local people add to the middle's projects through chipping in, raising money, and mindfulness crusades. The middle spotlights on establishing a strong climate for people with chemical imbalance and their families, offering instructive and helpful administrations.

The cooperative endeavors of experts, guardians, and volunteers from assorted foundations add to the progress of the Dubai Mental imbalance Community. This drive mirrors Dubai's commitment to inclusivity as well as features the city's endeavors to address the different requirements of its local area individuals.

Social Celebrations: Observing Variety

Dubai's schedule is dabbed with social celebrations that praise the variety of its inhabitants. The Emirates Aircraft Celebration of Writing, for example, unites writers, artists, and scholarly fans from around the world. The celebration effectively advances multifaceted exchange through abstract conversations, studios, and book signings.

Likewise, the Dubai Food Celebration is a gastronomic spectacle that features the different culinary practices of the city. Ostracizes and local people partake in the celebration, either as cooks, food lovers, or volunteers, adding to the festival of Dubai's multicultural culinary scene.

Chapter 9

"The Future Unveiled"

What was in store Revealed: Dubai's Visionary Direction

In the core of the Middle Eastern Landmass, where brilliant deserts meet the turquoise waters of the Bedouin Bay, Dubai remains as a signal of development, flexibility, and visionary authority. As the city has developed from an unobtrusive exchanging station to a worldwide city, its direction into what's to come has been set apart by nervy undertakings, key preparation, and a persistent quest for greatness. The tale of Dubai's future is one that unfurls at the crossing point of custom and innovation, desire and supportability, molding a cityscape that is both cutting edge and well established in its social legacy.

Key Metropolitan Preparation: Outline for Later

Dubai's horizon recounts the narrative of a city that opposes cutoff points and imagines a future where compositional wonders contact the sky. The vital metropolitan arranging that characterizes Dubai's scene is a demonstration of the city's obligation to practical development and innovation. The Dubai Plan 2021, a complete guide for the city's turn of events, incorporates six points of support, including a 'Shrewd and Practical City,' 'Imaginative and Enabled Individuals,' and 'Comprehensive and Firm Society.'

The visionary authority of Dubai perceives the significance of coordinating innovation, manageability, and personal satisfaction into the metropolitan texture. Drives like the Dubai Brilliant City project influence state of the art advancements like man-made consciousness, the Web of Things (IoT), and information investigation to upgrade proficiency, availability, and the in general metropolitan experience. As the city looks forward, these drives lay the foundation for a future where Dubai isn't simply a city however a residing, responsive living being.

Exhibition 2020: A Worldwide Grandstand of Development

At the junction of the past and what's in store stands Exhibition 2020 Dubai, a worldwide occasion that typifies the city's obligation to development, joint effort, and progress. Considered as a stage for countries to exhibit their accomplishments and dreams, Exhibition 2020 embodies Dubai's job as a worldwide center point for thoughts, business, and social trade.

The engineering of the Exhibition site itself is a demonstration of Dubai's cutting edge desires. The Manageability Structure, with its dynamic façade enlivened by the wings of a hawk, represents the congruity among nature and innovation. The Portability Structure, looking like a goliath wheel, connotes the interminable movement of progress. Through these famous designs, Exhibition 2020 isn't simply an occasion yet a brief look into the future — a future where maintainability, versatility, and development combine to shape a universe of potential outcomes.

Dubai 2040 Metropolitan End-all strategy: An Outline for Maintainable Development

As Dubai looks past Exhibition 2020, the as of late uncovered Dubai 2040 Metropolitan End-all strategy makes way for the city's proceeded with advancement. This aggressive outline imagines a city that focuses on maintainability, green spaces, and a harmony between metropolitan turn of events and normal scenes. The arrangement presents ideas like "Green Lung" regions, zeroing in on making interconnected stops and green spaces that improve the prosperity of occupants.

The obligation to reasonable portability is a foundation of the Dubai 2040 vision. The development of the metro organization, combination of independent vehicles, and accentuation on common well disposed metropolitan spaces highlight Dubai's assurance to decrease fossil fuel byproducts and make a city that is both productive and naturally cognizant. As the arrangement unfurls, Dubai positions itself as a city representing things to come as well as a worldwide model for supportable metropolitan living.

Mars Science City: Overcoming any issues Between Sci-fi and Reality

In a strong move that spans the domains of sci-fi and the truth, Dubai's Mars Science City is a visionary undertaking that looks to reproduce life on Mars. Imagined as a space for examination and trial and error, the city will highlight state of the art innovations, research centers, and reasonable living spaces that copy the states of the Red Planet.

This daring drive lines up with Dubai's obligation to space investigation and positions the city as a trailblazer in propelling humankind's compass past Earth.

The Mars Science City project mirrors Dubai's desire to add to logical headways and rouse people in the future. It embraces the soul of investigation as well as fills in as a demonstration of the city's capacity to transform aggressive ideas into unmistakable, noteworthy real factors.

Dubai Harbor: An Oceanic Desert garden of Extravagance and Development

Dubai Harbor, settled between Dubai Marina and Palm Jumeirah, is a waterfront improvement that exemplifies Dubai's sea desires. This venture imagines a refined mix of extravagance homes, a journey terminal, and a beacon enlivened Dubai Beacon that will act as a compositional milestone. The improvement likewise consolidates the Skydive Dubai region, supporting the city's obligation to adjusting entertainment and development.

Dubai Harbor's incorporation of supportable practices, like water protection and energy-productive plan, lines up with the city's obligation to mindful metropolitan turn of events. The undertaking grows Dubai's impression as well as improves the cityscape with a contemporary oceanic objective that lines up with the future-forward vision of Dubai.

Dubai's Vision for Man-made reasoning: A Mental Future

Dubai's excursion into what's in store is entwined with the combination of computerized reasoning (artificial intelligence) into different parts of metropolitan life. The city's initiative imagines a future where simulated intelligence improves productivity, smoothes out administrations, and changes the city into a worldwide man-made intelligence center point. The Dubai simulated intelligence Guide, sent off as a feature of the Dubai 2040 vision, frames a smart course of action for propelling man-made intelligence drives across areas like medical care, training, and transportation.

From computer based intelligence controlled client assistance cooperations to brilliant city arrangements that improve asset usage, Dubai is at the very front of embracing the mental future. The obligation to artificial intelligence innovative work positions the city as a worldwide forerunner in saddling innovation to address complex difficulties and work on the general personal satisfaction for its occupants.

Hydrogen Economy: Spearheading Feasible Energy Arrangements

Dubai's vision for what's in store stretches out past customary energy sources, with an essential spotlight on spearheading reasonable arrangements. The Green Hydrogen Undertaking, sent off as a feature of the Dubai Clean Energy Procedure 2050, plans to create and use green hydrogen as a perfect and environmentally friendly power source. This drive positions Dubai as a leader in the worldwide change towards a hydrogen economy, encouraging development and adding to the decrease of fossil fuel byproducts.

The Green Hydrogen Task lines up with Dubai's obligation to accomplishing 75% clean energy by 2050 and differentiating its energy blend. By putting resources into supportable advancements, the city isn't just getting its energy future yet additionally assuming a urgent part in the worldwide change to cleaner, more manageable energy sources.

Dubai's Social Vision: Supporting Legacy in a Cutting edge City

As Dubai impels itself into the future, it remains well established in its social legacy, safeguarding customs and cultivating a feeling of personality. The Dubai Culture 2025 well thought out course of action frames the city's vision for social turn of events, stressing the significance of imagination, variety, and inclusivity. Drives like Al Shindagha Exhibition hall and the Dubai Architecturally significant area highlight Dubai's obligation to supporting its social heritage in the midst of quick modernization.

The Exhibition hall Representing things to come, a notable construction that obscures the lines among engineering and innovation, is a demonstration of Dubai's commitment to cultivating development while praising its rich social embroidery. By mixing custom with innovation, the city plans to make a social scene that reverberates with occupants and guests the same, guaranteeing that Dubai's legacy stays a fundamental piece of its future story.

9.1 A glimpse into Dubai's ambitious future plans and projects.

A Brief look into Dubai's Aggressive Future: Visionary Undertakings and Groundbreaking Plans

Dubai, the gem of the Center East, isn't happy with just being a worldwide city; it tries to shape the fate of metropolitan living. As the sun sets on the transcending high rises that enhance its horizon, Dubai's vision stretches out a long ways into the great beyond, incorporating aggressive undertakings and groundbreaking plans that guarantee to rethink the cityscape. From reasonable megaprojects to notable mechanical progressions, this brief look into Dubai's aggressive future uncovers a story of development, supportability, and a steady quest for greatness.

Dubai Reasonable City: A Diagram for Green Metropolitan Living

In a strong move towards an economical future, Dubai Supportable City arises as an outlook changing venture. Settled on the edges of the city, this reason fabricated local area consolidates development, innovation, and ecological cognizance to make an agreeable harmony between metropolitan living and nature. With highlights like sunlight based chargers, green rooftops, and a strong waste reusing framework, Dubai Feasible City sets another norm for eco-accommodating metropolitan turn of events.

The people group's obligation to manageable transportation is exemplified by the broad organization of cycling ways and the combination of electric vehicles. Occupants of Dubai Economical City not just partake in a green desert spring in the core of the desert yet additionally add to the city's bigger vision of decreasing its biological impression. This task is a demonstration of Dubai's devotion to spearheading supportable arrangements that can be imitated on a worldwide scale.

Al Maktoum Worldwide Air terminal: Changing Dubai into a Flying Center point

As Dubai's worldwide importance keeps on taking off, the extension of Al Maktoum Global Air terminal arises as a basic part of the city's tentative arrangements. Arranged inside Dubai World Focal, this air terminal is ready to turn into the biggest on the planet upon fulfillment. The development not just obliges the developing number of guests to Dubai yet additionally positions the city as a significant worldwide flight center.

Al Maktoum Global Air terminal's essential area, joined with cutting edge offices and creative innovations, highlights Dubai's obligation to staying at the front line of the flight business. The undertaking not just mirrors the city's aggressive way to deal with framework advancement yet in addition lines up with its more extensive vision of working with worldwide network and cultivating monetary development.

Dubai Harbor: A Sea Symbol Rethinking Beach front Living

Dubai Harbor, arranged at the junction of extravagance and development, is an oceanic spectacle that adds one more layer to Dubai's aggressive future. This waterfront advancement rethinks seaside living as well as incorporates state of the art innovation and maintainability standards. With the Dubai Beacon as its highlight — a compositional wonder remaining as an image of sea progress — Dubai Harbor flags the city's obligation to pushing the limits of what is conceivable.

The voyage terminal inside Dubai Harbor positions the city as a critical objective for worldwide travels, drawing in sightseers and adding to the city's monetary enhancement. The task flawlessly mixes sporting spaces, extravagance homes, and nautical foundation, offering a brief look into Dubai's vision for an all encompassing and dynamic metropolitan experience that orchestrates with its beach front climate.

Gallery Representing things to come: Where Development and Custom Unite

The Gallery Representing things to come, a famous construction that challenges ordinary structural standards, epitomizes Dubai's obligation to being a worldwide place for development and information. This cutting edge wonder coordinates vanguard plan with best in class innovation, making a space where development and custom meet. Situated close the notorious Burj Khalifa, the historical center fills in as a guide for the people who try to figure out the crossing point of innovation, culture, and humankind.

As a demonstration of Dubai's desire to be a worldwide center point for innovative work, the Gallery Representing things to come isn't simply an actual space yet an impetus for extraordinary thoughts. With an emphasis on man-made consciousness, mechanical technology, and vivid innovations, the exhibition hall pushes Dubai into the cutting edge of the Fourth Modern Upset. It is an image of the city's unflinching conviction that development is the foundation of a prosperous future.

Dubai Metro Red Line Augmentation: Extending Network

Dubai's obligation to proficient and manageable transportation takes a jump forward with the expansion of the Dubai Metro Red Line. This aggressive task looks to interface key regions inside the city, upgrading openness, decreasing gridlock, and advancing practical metropolitan portability. The expansion mirrors Dubai's commitment to giving elite public transportation foundation that lines up with the city's vision for a more astute and more associated future.

The mix of trend setting innovations, like driverless trains, and the accentuation on making person on foot amicable spaces add to the by and large metropolitan experience. By growing the range of the metro organization, Dubai not just addresses the quick transportation needs of its inhabitants yet in addition lays the preparation for a more coordinated and earth cognizant city.

Dubai South: A Dream for Incorporated Metropolitan Living

Dubai South, an expert arranged city incorporating private, business, and modern zones, arises as a plan for coordinated metropolitan living. This visionary venture expects to make a self-supported local area that blends with its environmental elements while taking special care of the different requirements of its inhabitants. From Exhibition 2020 Dubai to Al Maktoum Global Air terminal, Dubai South decisively positions itself at the nexus of key turns of events, cultivating monetary development and local area commitment.

The undertaking's obligation to manageability is obvious in its green spaces, eco-accommodating foundation, and energy-proficient plan. Dubai South represents the city's extension as well as fills in as a demonstration of devotion to establishing all encompassing metropolitan conditions focus on personal satisfaction, monetary success, and ecological obligation.

The Green Hydrogen Task: A Jump Towards Clean Energy

In an earth shattering drive that places Dubai at the very front of the worldwide energy change, the Green Hydrogen Undertaking unfurls as a signal of supportable practices. As a component of the Dubai Clean Energy Procedure 2050, this task means to create green hydrogen utilizing environmentally friendly power sources, preparing for a cleaner and more supportable future. The accentuation on hydrogen as a spotless energy transporter mirrors Dubai's obligation to expanding its energy blend and diminishing fossil fuel byproducts.

The Green Hydrogen Venture positions Dubai as a trailblazer in the improvement of practical energy arrangements, with suggestions for the city as well as for the more extensive worldwide energy scene. By putting resources into state of the art advancements, Dubai reaffirms its job as a persuasive player in forming the eventual fate of clean energy.

Dubai's simulated intelligence Guide: Making ready for Mental Advancement

As computerized reasoning turns out to be progressively essential to the texture of present day cultures, Dubai uncovers its simulated intelligence Guide — a smart arrangement that frames the city's vision for saddling the force of man-made intelligence. From improving medical care administrations to reforming schooling and transportation, Dubai's artificial intelligence Guide positions the city as a pioneer in utilizing innovation to improve society.

The guide imagines a future where simulated intelligence is flawlessly coordinated into different parts of day to day existence, cultivating proficiency, development, and worked on nature of administrations. Dubai's obligation to propelling artificial intelligence lines up with its more extensive objective of turning into a worldwide center for mechanical development, mirroring the city's proactive way to deal with remaining ahead in the computerized time.

9.2 The role of technology, smart cities, and artificial intelligence.

The Job of Innovation, Shrewd Urban communities, and Man-made reasoning in Molding Dubai's Future

In the steadily developing scene of metropolitan turn of events, Dubai remains as a signal of mechanical development, embracing the groundbreaking force of savvy urban communities and computerized reasoning (simulated intelligence). As the city endeavors to turn into a worldwide forerunner in the computerized time, innovation isn't only a device however a main thrust behind Dubai's aggressive vision for what's in store. From savvy foundation to artificial intelligence driven administrations, this story investigates the crucial job of innovation in molding the city's direction.

Savvy Urban areas: Dubai's Vision for Shrewd Metropolitan Living

Dubai's excursion into what's in store is characteristically connected with the idea of brilliant urban communities — metropolitan conditions that influence innovation to improve the personal satisfaction for occupants, upgrade asset use, and make more reasonable networks. The Dubai Savvy City drive addresses a far reaching way to deal with incorporating state of the art innovations into the texture of the city, changing it into a no nonsense element that answers wisely to the requirements of its occupants.

One of the foundations of Dubai's brilliant city vision is the Dubai Information Drive. By tackling the force of information, the city means to further develop dynamic cycles, upgrade public administrations, and make a more consistent metropolitan experience.

Constant information examination empower specialists to address difficulties like gridlock, energy utilization, and waste administration, adding to a city that isn't simply productive yet additionally receptive to the unique necessities of its occupants.

Man-made reasoning: Forming the Mental Fate of Dubai

At the front line of Dubai's innovative development is the essential incorporation of man-made consciousness. The Dubai man-made intelligence Guide, sent off as a component of the Dubai 2040 vision, frames a far reaching plan for utilizing computer based intelligence across different areas. From medical care and training to transportation and public administrations, man-made intelligence is situated as an extraordinary power that upgrades productivity, development, and the general prosperity of Dubai's occupants.

One of the champion utilizations of man-made intelligence in Dubai is inside the medical services area. The Dubai Wellbeing System 2021 means to utilize man-made intelligence to foresee and forestall infections, customize treatment plans, and improve the general medical services insight. From simulated intelligence fueled demonstrative devices to prescient investigation that enhance emergency clinic work processes, Dubai's medical services framework is developing into a model of accuracy and productivity.

Dubai Web City: Cultivating a Tech Biological system

Settled inside the core of Dubai will be Dubai Web City (DIC), a mechanical desert spring that assumes an essential part in cultivating development and business venture.

Laid out in 1999, DIC has developed into an energetic local area of tech organizations, new businesses, and worldwide partnerships, making a synergistic environment that impels Dubai into the worldwide tech field.

DIC fills in as a demonstration of Dubai's obligation to establishing a climate where innovation flourishes. The Free Zone model executed in DIC works with a business-accommodating climate, drawing in tech monsters and arising new companies the same. The cooperative soul inside DIC adds to the city's more extensive story of mechanical headway, situating Dubai as a center for computerized development and information trade.

Shrewd Foundation: The Foundation of The upcoming Dubai

As Dubai keeps on developing upward and on a level plane, the job of shrewd framework turns out to be progressively essential. The Shrewd Dubai drive imagines a city where framework isn't simply physical however keen — equipped for adjusting to the necessities of its clients and streamlining functional effectiveness. From savvy matrices that oversee energy utilization to shrewd transportation frameworks that simplicity traffic stream, Dubai's foundation is developing into a refined organization of interconnected, information driven components.

One model of this savvy foundation is the Dubai Water Trench. Past its tasteful allure, the trench incorporates savvy innovations to oversee water stream, screen water quality, and improve by and large manageability. This ground breaking way to deal with metropolitan advancement guarantees that Dubai's foundation isn't just strong yet in addition lined up with the standards of natural awareness.

Simulated intelligence in Transportation: Exploring What's to come

Dubai's obligation to clever transportation is apparent in drives that saddle the force of simulated intelligence to upset the manner in which individuals move inside the city. The Dubai Independent Transportation Procedure plans to change 25% of the city's complete transportation into independent mode by 2030. From independent cabs to self-driving transports, computer based intelligence is reshaping the portability scene, offering a dream of a future where transportation isn't simply proficient yet in addition more secure and more practical.

The Streets and Transport Authority (RTA) has been a pioneer in embracing simulated intelligence inside the transportation area. The incorporation of simulated intelligence into traffic the board frameworks considers constant investigation of traffic designs, prompting versatile signs that streamline traffic stream. Moreover, computer based intelligence driven prescient upkeep upgrades the proficiency and dependability of public transportation administrations, adding to a consistent and innovatively progressed metropolitan portability experience.

Dubai Police: man-made intelligence Controlled Public Security

In a city where wellbeing and security are fundamental, Dubai Police has embraced man-made brainpower as a device to improve public wellbeing. The reception of artificial intelligence controlled advances, like facial acknowledgment and prescient policing, permits policing proactively address potential security dangers. The Savvy Police headquarters, furnished with man-made intelligence driven administrations, furnishes occupants with a scope of administrations, from revealing wrongdoings to paying fines, in a productive and innovation driven way.

Computer based intelligence likewise assumes a significant part in Dubai's endeavors to make a prescient and protection way to deal with public wellbeing. Overwhelmingly of information, man-made intelligence calculations can distinguish designs that might show likely crime, permitting policing mediate before episodes happen. This proactive methodology lines up with Dubai's more extensive vision of utilizing innovation to make a city where inhabitants have a real sense of safety and safeguarded.

Dubai's Vision for 5G: The Following Outskirts of Availability

As the world advances into the period of 5G innovation, Dubai is at the front of embracing the following wilderness of network.

The sending of 5G organizations across the city vows to upset correspondence, availability, and the Web of Things (IoT). With dramatically quicker information speeds and decreased inertness, 5G is an impetus for the multiplication of savvy gadgets and the consistent reconciliation of innovation into each part of metropolitan life.

The organization of 5G organizations improves the productivity of existing administrations as well as makes the way for additional opportunities. From savvy homes and associated vehicles to vivid increased reality encounters, Dubai's hug of 5G innovation positions the city as a residing research center for the capability of super quick, low-dormancy network.

9.3 Reflection on Dubai's position in the global landscape and its ongoing journey as a desert jewel.

Reflection on Dubai's Worldwide Standing: A Continuous Excursion as a Desert Gem

In the complex embroidery of the worldwide scene, Dubai arises as a stunning diamond in the core of the Middle Eastern Desert — a city that challenges shows, rises above limits, and consistently rethinks itself on the great phase of global unmistakable quality. Considering Dubai's situation on the planet inspires a story of versatility, desire, and the consistent combination of custom and innovation that impels the city into what's to come.

Worldwide Financial Center: Dubai's Brilliant Ascent

Dubai's fleeting ascent from a modest fishing and exchanging town to a worldwide financial force to be reckoned with is out and out remarkable. The city's essential area, settled between Europe, Asia, and Africa, has worked with its change into a basic center for exchange, trade, and money. The Dubai Worldwide Air terminal, a clamoring entryway interfacing mainlands, encapsulates the city's job as a worldwide flight and coordinated operations community.

As a demonstration of its financial ability, Dubai has set up a good foundation for itself as a flourishing business and venture objective. The formation of free zones, like the Dubai Global Monetary Center (DIFC) and the Jebel Ali Free Zone (JAFZA), has drawn in worldwide companies and worked with unfamiliar direct venture. The expansion of the economy, with a shift from oil reliance to areas like the travel industry, land, and innovation, has upgraded Dubai's versatility despite worldwide monetary variances.

Social Focal point: Custom in a Cutting edge City

Dubai's social character is a rich embroidery woven from strings of custom, legacy, and a steadfast obligation to inclusivity. The city's initiative perceives the significance of protecting its social roots in the midst of the quick rushes of modernization. Drives like the Al Shindagha Exhibition hall and the Dubai Historically significant area are strong tokens of Dubai's excursion from a pearl jumping town to a cosmopolitan city.

The Burj Khalifa, standing tall as a design wonder, and the customary souks, where the reverberations of bargaining have persevered through everyday hardship, exist next to each other, framing a novel juxtaposition of the old and the new. Dubai's devotion to facilitating widespread developments and celebrations, for example, the Dubai Shopping Celebration and the Dubai Food Celebration, further highlights its obligation to commending variety and encouraging a feeling of solidarity among its occupants and guests.

Structural Wonders: Horizon as a Material

Dubai's horizon is a famous demonstration of human inventiveness and engineering splendor, a demonstration of the city's bold soul and desire. The Burj Khalifa, puncturing the sky at north of 828 meters, remains as an image of Dubai's steady quest for significance. The Palm Jumeirah, a fake archipelago molded like a palm tree, epitomizes the city's capacity to reshape its geology for both stylish and down to earth purposes.

The cityscape of Dubai is a material where draftsmen and designers push the limits of what is conceivable. The Dubai Shopping center, the biggest shopping center on the planet, isn't simply a business space however a vivid encounter that consistently incorporates retail, diversion, and recreation. The Burj Al Middle Easterner, with its sail-formed outline, isn't simply a lavish inn yet a compositional symbol that graces postcards and travel leaflets around the world.

The travel industry Desert spring: Inviting the World

Dubai's charm as a travel industry desert spring is woven into its actual texture, welcoming guests from each edge of the globe to encounter its novel mix of lavishness and warmth. The city's obligation to making top notch attractions, like the Dubai Wellspring and the Dubai Show, lifts its status as a worldwide the travel industry area of interest. The yearly Exhibition 2020 Dubai, a festival of development and coordinated effort, further cements Dubai's situation as an objective for those looking for both relaxation and scholarly excitement.

The neighborliness area in Dubai is inseparable from extravagance, offering a variety of rich lodgings, resorts, and encounters that take care of the different preferences of a worldwide crowd. From the seven-star Burj Al Middle Easterner to the quiet desert resorts, Dubai's neighborliness industry sets a norm of greatness that reverberates with the city's obligation to giving a significant and unrivaled experience for its visitors.

Mechanical Vanguard: A City Representing things to come

Dubai's introduction to what's to come is portrayed by its hug of state of the art innovation, situating itself as a city at the very front of development. The Savvy Dubai drive, incorporating man-made brainpower, information examination, and the Web of Things, changes the city into a living research center for shrewd metropolitan living. The Dubai Web City, a flourishing tech biological system, encourages development and business, adding to the city's story as a worldwide tech center point.

The obligation to feasible practices is exemplified by the Green Hydrogen Undertaking, a spearheading drive in the domain of clean energy. Dubai's essential vision for a hydrogen-fueled future not just positions the city as a forerunner in maintainability yet in addition highlights its assurance to assume an imperative part in the worldwide progress to sustainable power sources.

A Green Desert garden in the Desert: Supportability In the midst of the Sands

Dubai's obligation to manageability challenges the cliché picture of a desert city, changing it into a green desert spring through aggressive finishing and natural drives. The Green Dubai project, zeroing in on upgrading green spaces and metropolitan biodiversity, represents the city's commitment to establishing a maintainable and eco-accommodating climate. The Al Marmoom Protection Hold, a tremendous span of safeguarded desert scene, remains as a demonstration of Dubai's work to offset metropolitan improvement with ecological conservation.

The Dubai Trench, wandering through the city, isn't just an accomplishment of designing yet additionally an exhibit of Dubai's obligation to water protection and maintainable metropolitan preparation. The city's initiative perceives that an amicable conjunction with nature is significant for long haul practicality, and Dubai's continuous endeavors to battle environmental change and safeguard its regular legacy mirror a comprehensive way to deal with feasible turn of events.

Comprehensive Tomorrow: Resilience as a Support point

One of the central attributes of Dubai's worldwide personality is its obligation to resistance and inclusivity. In a city where more than 200 ethnicities coincide agreeably, Dubai remains as a brilliant illustration of variety celebrated and contrasts embraced. The foundation of the Dubai Resilience Grant and the facilitating of occasions like the World Resistance Culmination highlight the city's devotion to encouraging a climate where individuals of different societies, religions, and foundations live and cooperate in harmony.

Dubai's receptiveness to alternate points of view is reflected in the concurrence of mosques, holy places, temples, and sanctuaries, representing the city's hug of strict variety. The Extended period of Resilience in 2019 further cemented Dubai's obligation to advancing comprehension and acknowledgment on a worldwide scale, making way for a future where solidarity and regard are essential standards.